THE SHAKLEE STORY

Books by Robert L. Shook

The Shaklee Story

The Chief Executive Officers

The Real Estate People

The Entrepreneurs

Ten Greatest Salespersons

Why Didn't I Think of That?

Winning Images

Successful Telephone Selling in the '80s
(with Martin D. Shafiroff)

How to Be the Complete Professional Salesman
(with Herbert Shook)

Total Commitment
(with Ronald Bingamen)

THE
SHAKLEE
STORY

ROBERT L. SHOOK

1817

HARPER & ROW, PUBLISHERS, New York
Cambridge, Philadelphia, San Francisco, London
Mexico City, São Paulo, Sydney

FIRST EDITION

Designer: Sidney Feinberg

Library of Congress Cataloging in Publication Data

Shook, Robert L., 1938–
  The Shaklee story.
    1. Shaklee Corporation. 2. Shaklee, Forrest Clell.
3. Businessmen—United States—Biography. 4. Direct
selling—United States. I. Title.
HD9503.U54S477 1982   381   81–48155
ISBN 0–06–015005–X   AACR2

---

82 83 84 85 86 10 9 8 7 6 5 4 3 2 1

*This book is dedicated to my father, in honor
of his 70th birthday*

Acknowledgments

I am very grateful to my editor, Irv Levey; his assistant, Daniel Bial; and to my assistant, Jeanne Desy. The writing of *The Shaklee Story* was more than the work of an individual author—it was a team effort.

I gratefully acknowledge Shaklee's Master Coordinators, without whom there would be no *Shaklee Story:* J. K. & Rebecca Baker, Earl & Martha Bates, Robert & Constance Bergeth, Harold & Audrey Bergquist, Earl & JoAnn Boltinghouse, James & Delphae Boyd, Lee & Mary Breatchel, Gary & Faye Burke, James & Mary Jo Burke, Edward & Aurora Cano, Jack & Bonnie Cranney, Naomi Cranney, Raymond & Susan De-Brincat, Dick & Carol Dinkel, Richard & Cleo Dunlap, Ross & Mary Margaret Earley, Bob & Pat Ewing, Roger & Mary Jo Ewing, Floyd & Betty Farner, Frank & Cindy Frey, Harry & Lorraine Frisch, Bill & Claire Gardner, Bill & Mary Jo Geideck, Jack & Margarita Gerristen, Bob & Diane Giddens, John & Tressie Goetz, Paul & Ruth Hallberg, Al & Joan Hegerman, Lee & Linda Hershberger, Chuck & Joyce Hoffman, Bob & Kay Holker, Leon & Joycelyn Huisman, Del & Joanne Johannsen, Roy & Sandra Kessler, Gene & Arlene Libby, James &

Shirley Longnecker, Gary & Mary Loomis, Roy & Frances Madsen, Bruce & Elaine Mannes, Dix & Bunny Martin, Sylvia E. McMichael, Leon & Ellyn Naef, Harry & Ruth Nichols, Roger & Norma Olsen, Roland & Mary Oosterhouse, Norman & Mary Ann Pahmeier, Leon & Shirley Pemberton, Hewey & Bette Peterson, Herbert & Edith Price, Carlos & Teresa Ramos, Doug & Gloria Sandberg, Darrell & Flo Satterfield, Dave & Val Setterholm, Don & Pat Simecka, Robert & Bernice Sis, Don & Carolyn Spargur, Dave & Ellie Stoltzfus, James & Carole Stubbs, Pat & Jeanne Wherley.

—ROBERT L. SHOOK

Contents

Acknowledgments   7

Preface   11

1. Forrest C. Shaklee—The Man   15

2. The Early Years   33

3. The World's Greatest Sales Organization   49

4. Shaklee International   65

5. The Best Investment Ever Made (*The Hegerman Story*)   75

6. The Greatest Self-Improvement Program in the
   World (*The Spargur Story*)   89

7. The Rewards of Persistence (*The Simecka Story*)   101

8. "Behind Every Successful Woman . . ."
   (*The Boltinghouse Story*)   115

9. A Japanese Love Affair (*The Ara Story*)   127

10. Think Big! (*The Holker Story*)   135

11. The Sharing and Caring Corporation   151

12. Where Nature and Know-How Join Hands   161

13. Shaklee, Today and Tomorrow   175

Appendix: The Shaklee Sales Organization and Sales Plan   185

Illustrations follow pages 64 and 128

Preface

As I complete this manuscript the Shaklee Corporation is celebrating its Silver Jubilee. In the twenty-five years since it was founded by Dr. Forrest Shaklee and his sons, Forrest, Jr., and Raleigh, the company has become a nearly half-billion-dollar enterprise, listed on the New York Stock Exchange and committed to international expansion. This company, founded with almost no assets but the absolute conviction of the Shaklees and a single high-quality product, is living proof that an American Dream can still come true. Shaklee's sales structure, through which independent Distributors build their own businesses with the help of the parent company, exemplifies the unparalleled opportunities the American free enterprise system can offer. In researching this book I uncovered the stories of many representatives who started from scratch and built their own Shaklee organizations that have given them a financial independence beyond their dreams.

A major portion of this book is given to the stories of six husband-wife teams—a cross section of representatives who have attained the highest rank in the Shaklee field organization. There are countless other stories, each unique, and of course it is impossible to write about them all. But these chapters will help you identify with real people—and they *are* Shaklee. For while *The Shaklee Story* is about a business enterprise, it is also about individuals in a very people-oriented company.

The Shaklee story is especially appropriate for the 1980s. In recent years Americans have become increasingly health-conscious and aware of the nutritional inadequacy of processed and convenience foods. This interest in nutrition, I believe, is here to stay; and as more people around the world need or choose to supplement their diets, the Shaklee Corporation will continue to grow. "Timing is everything," as they say in business; and Shaklee, with its fine management team and its productive organization, seems on the threshold of tremendous growth. As the company's sales volume continues to soar, it seems likely that Shaklee will become a household word not just in the United States but in numerous countries throughout the world.

In writing this book, I received an unexpected bonus. While I have always been committed to maintaining my health through exercise, I had never given any thought to nutrition, assuming that if I ate three meals a day I was getting what I needed. As I studied Shaklee and learned about nutritional supplementation, I became interested enough to begin taking Shaklee products. Even as I did this, I reserved my judgment, for I had always felt good—but I didn't know how good I *could* feel! More than any facts and figures could, my personal experience convinced me of the importance of good nutrition. I became a Shaklee believer!

I am very grateful for the cooperation extended to me by Shaklee executives. Without hesitation—in fact, with pride—they opened all their doors so that I could examine every aspect of the company. The end result is a multifaceted story about nutrition, about a corporation that combines free enterprise with real concern and incentives for its people, and about the opportunities still available today within our American system. This is *The Shaklee Story*.

THE SHAKLEE STORY

1

Forrest C. Shaklee—The Man

THE STORY of Dr. Forrest Shaklee is not the typical Horatio Alger story. True, he went from rags to riches and from disappointment to fulfillment while still a young man; but his greatest accomplishment, the one that brought him the most money and fame, didn't occur until many years later. In 1956, at age sixty-two, he came out of retirement to develop an unusual line of products and a unique selling system that was to become—there is no other way to put it—a phenomenal success.

So this is not a story of overnight success or beginner's luck. Dr. Shaklee had already met with success in numerous previous enterprises. He was a prosperous chiropractor. He was an inventor and research scientist. He was a published author, having written books on business, philosophy, and psychology. He was a radio personality, preaching theology both on the air and in the church where he acted as pastor. He was a businessman, an entrepreneur, a showman: in short, an original.

Despite the seeming diversity of all these endeavors, the talents that went into making each a success were the same as those directly responsible for the early success of the Shaklee Corporation. Shaklee drew on his knowledge of science—

which he had developed in his work as chiropractor, research scientist, and inventor; on his knowledge of business—which he had developed as an entrepreneur; and on his ability to communicate—which he had developed in his work as orator, preacher, author, and showman. His ability to get things done, to see things through, had been developed during all of his previous endeavors, but the Shaklee Corporation would draw upon his talents as nothing had before. This ability was the result of firm moral, philosophical, and religious convictions that allowed him to feel secure with himself, with the world, and with all that he did. One other talent that stood him in good stead was his excellence as a father, for he raised two sons who were also vitally related to the success of the Shaklee Corporation.

Forrest Shaklee was born in November 1894 in Carlisle, Iowa, the second son of indigent farmers. The midwife attending the birth immediately diagnosed consumption (tuberculosis), and the doctors called in later concurred. The baby could not be expected to live long. Observing the child's labored breathing, one doctor said that his short life would be a "living death."

The only treatment at the time for tuberculosis was good food, fresh air, and lots of rest. The family moved from the soot and smoke of the Carlisle coal mines to a farm near Moorland in northern Iowa. Progress was slow, however, and all of Forrest's childhood was that of a convalescent, with long afternoons of solitary bed rest.

On sunny days the boy spent much of his time out of doors wandering around the fields. He spent long hours alone, observing nature and thinking. Lying quietly on an old haystack, he watched animals in their natural environment and he speculated about the unseen force that guided migrating birds, and about the instincts that led a sentinel crow to warn the wild ducks when a hunter approached. Most of all he was fascinated by the acute senses and instincts of farm animals. Long before he could detect an impending storm, the sows in the barnyard would gather husks and straw to make warm beds in their pens. "Animals listen to the voice of Nature," he realized, "while men have forgotten how."

As Forrest spent so much time out of doors, he was frequently asked to gather plants and herbs that his mother and her friends used in preparing folk remedies. He gathered ground ivy, catnip, dandelion, chicory, curled dock, burgamot, joe-pye weed, wild cherry, goldenrod, and wild ginger. These he helped brew into teas, mix in salads, or use in the creation of liniment or tonic.

The boy learned what the man would need to know: how to turn a setback into an advantage. Forrest did not allow his illness to ruin his life. The time he spent alone he used— developing disciplinary muscles, sharpening his sense of observation, and learning to think rationally and usefully.

Nature he observed most, and he came to respect it greatly. Not surprisingly, he was most fascinated with the healing powers of nature. Nature has the ability to kill and to heal, he realized, but nature's ways of death were far more understandable than its power to heal. How did nature heal? Was living in harmony with nature the key? Is it *possible* to live in harmony with nature in the twentieth century?

By the time he was a teenager, Forrest was "attuned to the signs of Nature's revelations." The solitary summers out of doors had laid the foundation for the philosophy he would develop as a mature man. By this time, also, his health had improved remarkably. He was able to ride his bicycle everywhere, to run with his dog, and to spend more time each day active and less time lying in the sun. Finally the doctors were satisfied that his tuberculosis had been arrested.

Still the teenager was frail compared to most other boys his age. Concerned about his development, Forrest's father introduced him to *Physical Culture,* the magazine of Bernarr Macfadden's health empire. Forrest was challenged by Macfadden's ideas, and he exercised every day, even trying to emulate Macfadden by lifting newborn calves over his head.

(Macfadden was legendary for performing this feat with larger animals.)

Macfadden believed in an intimate relationship between the health of the body, general vitality, intelligence, and good nutrition. He inveighed against refined white flour, sugar, and the overconsumption of salt. In accordance, Forrest revised his diet—although the evidence that supported this theory was not found until many years later.

Macfadden also believed that drugs often mask the symptom without curing the disease. He was certain that heart patients and consumptives needed to exercise to regain their health. Forrest knew firsthand how exercise contributed to his recovery from consumption. He had devoted himself so fully to physical culture that when Macfadden visited the area to give a demonstration, Forrest was chosen to assist in the show.

Forrest discovered a streak of chicanery in Macfadden and was disappointed in the man who once had meant so much to him. Nevertheless, Macfadden's ideas had a lasting influence on Forrest, and he remained convinced of the basic value of these ideas.

While still a teenager Forrest became interested in the use of hypnosis to cure the sick. He went to see a hypnotist and psychologist appearing in nearby Rock Island, Illinois, who went by the name of Professor Santinelli. When Santinelli asked for a volunteer to be hypnotized, Forrest shot up his hand. He proved such a good subject for the hypnotist's demonstration that Santinelli asked the youth to assist him for the rest of the tour.

The few months Forrest spent touring with Santinelli were by and large uneventful. One night, however, as Forrest sat in the audience paying little attention to the lecture that preceded the demonstration, he was startled to hear Santinelli shout, "What you think, you look. What you think, you do. What you think, you are!" The meaning of this suddenly flashed in Forrest's mind. This message became important later in Forrest's own philosophy of active, positive thinking.

Shortly thereafter, Forrest met the great American orator and politician William Jennings Bryan. As he crossed the country making his Chautauqua speeches, Bryan stayed with farm families; the Shaklees were his hosts more than once. The boy was awestruck by the dynamic speaker, who had come from a farm background like Forrest's own. One day Robert Shaklee found his son in a field delivering a speech to an invisible audience, arms flying, just like his hero Bryan. Forrest explained that he wanted to develop his powers of elocution and persuasion.

Robert, a staunch Republican, admired Bryan but did not share his Democratic views. "It's all right for you to speak like him, son," he replied, "but don't think like him."

Politics aside, Forrest learned some important lessons from Bryan. Although Bryan was an imposing figure, he knew sincere humility and was able to laugh at himself. This came as a revelation to the hero-worshipping young man. In addition to interesting Forrest in the art of public speaking, Bryan, by example, encouraged the young man to learn how to laugh at himself.

It was evident as Forrest grew older that he would never be a farmer. When he began to ponder his life's work, he quickly narrowed his consideration to the health care fields. Since he knew he wanted to treat people on the most natural basis, naturopathic medicine appealed to him; this branch had been developed from folk medicine and stressed treatment through natural substances. Forrest was also influenced by Bernarr Macfadden's teaching that "the secret of human power lies in the spinal cord, the brain, and the nervous system generally." Knowing that the growing science of chiropractic centered on adjustments to the vertebrae, Forrest was very interested in this field. A dramatic personal experience decided the issue for him.

When Forrest, now in his late teens, experienced severe abdominal and back pains, doctors in Patterson and neighboring Indianola diagnosed appendicitis. Unconvinced, Forrest asked to be taken to see Dr. McGinnis, a chiropractor in Rockwell City.

"What if he agrees that it's appendicitis?" Robert Shaklee asked his son.

"Then I'll have the operation."

Dr. McGinnis did not agree with the diagnosis. Instead he found a vertebra out of its normal position that was causing pressure on the nerve of the lower right abdomen. The treatment, without drugs or surgery, was entirely successful. Once the vertebra was back in position, the pain disappeared. To this day, Forrest has his appendix.

Forrest was won over to this natural form of healing. ("Chiropractic," which comes from the Greek, means "hands, used effectively.") He enrolled in the Palmer School of Chiropractic in Davenport, Iowa. Joshua Bartlett Palmer, a brilliant and aggressive young man, ran the school founded by his father. Forrest admired Palmer and agreed with his holistic approach: "Health does not come merely by taking medicine or making structural adjustments. . . . The individual must obey the laws of Nature."

However, Forrest's admiration for J. B. Palmer was qualified; Palmer was obsessed with the idea that chiropractic was the only useful treatment for physical disorders. Forrest had observed and read enough to know that a more encompassing system was needed to preserve health. At the Palmer School he saw that many individuals who came in for treatment were undernourished, though often overfed. He came to believe that, though there was no single key to health and vitality, poor nutrition was a central cause of *dis*-ease (as chiropractic usually called it). In his own practice, he vowed, he would always be conscious of the importance of diet in maintaining health.

After Forrest was graduated in June 1915, he went to visit his parents, meaning to stop only briefly first to see Dr. McGinnis in Rockwell City. There he found the answer to his unresolved future: Dr. McGinnis wanted to sell his practice and equipment. The whole package was a bargain at five thousand dollars—except that Forrest had only seventy-eight dollars to his name. Holding his breath he asked, "Would you consider taking one thousand?" Dr. McGinnis said he would.

Now Forrest had only to find the thousand dollars, quite a large sum at the time. From Dr. McGinnis's office he went to the First National Bank. The manager listened with interest to the beginning chiropractor's dreams for the practice, but he had to ask the inevitable question: "What collateral can you provide?"

Since the obvious answer was "none," Forrest sat silent for a moment. The banker began to grow impatient; the young man looked like just another poor risk.

Then, with quiet confidence, Forrest tapped his forehead and said, "My collateral is up here."

The banker pondered for a moment. He took a long, hard look at Forrest, and then he smiled. "I'm sure you'll make good. Will you sign here, Dr. Shaklee?" Thus the loan was approved.

At first, business was slow, but Forrest was able to use his spare time profitably. Whenever he was not seeing patients, he could be found in his laboratory. At the Palmer School he had witnessed experiments in nutrition. Mice, rabbits, and guinea pigs were given large doses of minerals, and they showed new signs of health relative to the amount and kind of mineral taken. Forrest continued experimenting, focusing on how certain foods related to overall health.

The young doctor's interest in the new field of nutrition carried over to his work with patients. Unlike other doctors of the time, he questioned his patients closely about the food they consumed, and he devised detailed charts to monitor their progress. After studying these records, he was convinced that those individuals who included fresh vegetables in their diets recovered their good health more quickly.

When he left his lab at night, Forrest often read scientific journals until the small hours of the morning. He was especially fascinated by articles on the work of Casimir Funk, a Polish biochemist who, in 1912, had isolated natural substances he called "vitamines." Forrest himself had been working on techniques for processing these vital organic compounds; he called the tablets he had compounded, "vitalized minerals."

Forrest wrote to the famed biochemist, and when Funk answered they began a correspondence on their research. Though they were working on the same problems, the two had different approaches. Funk was involved in pure research, while Forrest's concern was practical.

The credit for the discovery of vitamins goes to Funk, although Forrest's discoveries were practically simultaneous. The coincidence of having two people make similar discoveries at the same time is not uncommon in science. Forrest took solace in Elbert Hubbard's pragmatic philosophy: "There is no such thing as an original idea. It is simply an idea whose time has come."

In December of that year Forrest married Ruth Chapin, whom he had met at a church function. It was clear to the bride from the moment the young couple arrived in Rockwell City following their honeymoon that her husband's practice would always be demanding. They were met at the railroad depot by a farmer whose wife needed medical attention, and instead of going home the newlyweds rode in a horse and buggy over the snow to the farmhouse.

In November 1917 Ruth gave birth to their first son, Forrest Clell Shaklee, Jr. A few months later the young family moved to Fort Dodge, thirty miles from Rockwell City. Here Forrest ambitiously opened a facility that incorporated various specialties of medicine. In addition to a fifteen-bed sanatorium, the offices contained thirty-two treatment rooms. He hired a staff that included not only chiropractors but osteopaths, internists, general practitioners, and surgeons. In the sanatorium, Forrest kept patients on vitamin-rich diets while he assessed individual needs for dietary supplements. The clinic soon became busy and prosperous.

Although the clinic was thriving, many of Forrest's patients were unable to travel from the country to Fort Dodge, so he continued making house calls. This was a difficult and time-consuming part of his practice. In 1918, when the major mode of transportation was still the horse and buggy, the young doctor purchased and flew a two-passenger Curtis airplane, one that could land in a patient's field. While Forrest may not have been the first flying doctor in the United States, he was certainly the first in Iowa, and soon his landings were cheered by excited crowds.

In addition to serving as administrator of his clinic, Forrest spent a great deal of time in X-ray diagnosis. At the time, the hazards of excessive exposure to X rays were not fully known, and the precautionary measures were not as effective as those taken today. In 1921, concerned about severe ulcerating burns on his left shoulder and left hip, Forrest consulted a cancer specialist in Chicago.

As he feared, the diagnosis was cancer. The doctor said the arm would have to be amputated to the shoulder.

"What about my hip?" Forrest asked.

"Your leg will also have to be amputated up to the hip."

The specialist went on to say that even with amputation the carcinoma might be halted for only a few months.

At the specialist's urging, Forrest agreed to visit the famed Mayo Clinic in Rochester, Minnesota. The diagnosis was the same: only amputation could arrest the spread of the cancer.

In the train on the way home Forrest considered the future that had been painted for him. His thoughts turned again and again to his son and young wife, who was expecting another child. By the time he reached home he had made a decision. The cancer would not cut his life short, and he would not become a helpless amputee.

"I *will* live," he told Ruth. "I will heal. I know I can do it." With these strong words, Forrest made a deep commitment to act on his belief in the healing power of Nature. He'd bet his life on it.

Within a few weeks he sold the clinic and moved the family back to Davenport, Iowa. There he began an intensive program of nutrition, continual blood analysis, and occasional fasting. In order to have the freshest, most nourishing diet, he regularly drove to the countryside, where he purchased fruits and vegetables from farmers the same day they were picked. This diet he supplemented with large quantities of vitamins and minerals.

For several months the ulcerated sores on his shoulder and hip showed no improvement; Forrest suffered enormous pain. Yet he was certain that his healing depended on his positive conviction that he *would* heal; he never let that conviction waver. On December 2, 1921, he had still another incentive to live. His second son, Raleigh (nicknamed Lee), was born.

As the months passed, Forrest and Ruth detected a slow but steady improvement; the ulcerated sores began to heal. By the end of 1922 they had been replaced by healthy tissue, and Forrest had regained the strength and energy of full health. Not only was he alive and well again, but the defeat of the illness convinced him that his ideas on nutrition were absolutely sound. He was more certain than ever that good nutrition could help other people too.

In spite of Forrest's dramatic cure, medical specialists remained skeptical. When Forrest visited the Chicago clinic he was told the cancer was only in remission. Similarly, the Mayo Clinic, while impressed by the "remission," had no intention of pursuing Forrest's theories about why healthy cells had been able to defeat carcinogenic cells.

The nutritional cure was not a simple one, Forrest agreed. First, when he contracted the illness he had been a basically healthy person; that was a highly significant factor. Second, he had followed a diet he thought would best fit his needs.

Because individuals are unique, "we must approach ourselves and our needs accordingly." Certainly there was no one standard dietary program which could be applied uniformly to treat disease. The dramatic cure fueled his fervor to learn more and more about the natural way to health.

In July 1924, fully recovered, Forrest opened the Shaklee Clinic in Mason City, Iowa. Here for the first time his formulations for food supplements were packaged and dispensed to patients with nutritional deficiencies. Forrest headed what may have been the largest clinic of its kind in the world at the time.

Through the late 1920s the Shaklee Clinic prospered, as had Forrest's earlier practices. During evening office hours Forrest, Jr., and Lee frequently worked beside him in his laboratory, filling capsules and packaging bottles of the nutritional supplements Forrest gave his patients.

In Mason City, Forrest became very active in the Christian Church. He was so respected for his knowledge of theology and his ability to inspire that he was asked to deliver a series of sermons. He possessed a commanding platform presence and a resonant, expressive voice. As the series went on, his reputation spread, and attendance at the church grew.

Forrest's sermons were so popular that when a sister church in Portland, Iowa, had a vacancy he was asked to fill in full time on Sunday mornings while the elders conducted a search for a new pastor. When the time finally came to vote for a candidate, Forrest was surprised to hear that he had been unanimously chosen. For, while he had completed studies for a doctor of divinity degree, he had never been ordained. In January 1929 the elders ordained Forrest as a minister. Four years later he officially received his doctor of divinity degree.

In 1929 a chance event sent Forrest's life in a new direction. The Cerro Gordo Hotel, where his offices were located, caught fire. All his furniture, equipment, and records were lost, but the greatest loss was his personal files, which had contained his correspondence with William Jennings Bryan and Casimir Funk, among others. Everything burned except a personally inscribed set of Elbert Hubbard's *Little Journeys*. Forrest found the little inspirational books the next morning. "It was as if Elbert Hubbard was telling me, 'When all else is destroyed, only the product of the mind persists.' "

Since he was well insured, Forrest could afford to open new offices. But the fire allowed him to consider his future. He decided he wanted to devote his full efforts to nutritional research; his interest was increasingly focused on building good health rather than treating sick patients.

Forrest decided, however, he needed a vacation first. He had worked without a vacation for the fourteen years since graduation. He decided to take his family to Florida. For the long journey he had built what he called a "touring home"— a clinic truck remodeled to form a house. This forerunner of the camper included bunks, a closet for fishing rods, an ice box, a gasoline stove, and running water in a storage tank.

The odd vehicle had another significant innovation—synthetic rubber tires made from Forrest's formula. Forrest's interest in synthetic rubber had been inspired by the reported experiments of Thomas Edison, Henry Ford, and Harvey Firestone, who were attempting to find or develop a latex-bearing plant that could be grown in the United States. Forrest believed that concept was impractical and set out to create a rubberlike compound made entirely of synthetics.

In long, late hours in his laboratory, he tried and discarded one formula after another until he produced a substance with most of the characteristics of natural rubber. To test the compound further he ordered tire molds made to his specifications, and used the molds to produce tires for his car and the clinic truck. When he was satisfied that the tires were durable, he hired an attorney to begin a patent search. The search would take time, he was told. Satisfied that he had gone as far as he could with this project, Forrest turned his attention to other things.

In 1929 the Shaklees set out for Florida in their unusual camper with its synthetic tires. In Florida crowds gathered around to gawk at the strange vehicle. The crowds attracted newsmen, who noticed the unusual tires. They asked Forrest if he was in Fort Myers to join Edison, Firestone, and Ford, who were meeting at Edison's estate to discuss their experiments with synthetic rubber. Forrest admitted that the tires were his own invention, and that he hadn't even known about the meeting. In another of the coincidences common in scientific research, Harvey Firestone had already filed a patent for synthetic rubber.

The next morning, after the papers came out with a feature story about the touring home, Forrest received an invitation from Edison for lunch and a game of golf. Forrest accepted quickly.

While the golf game was mediocre ("Edison was shooting in the 190s," Forrest recalls), the conversation over lunch was memorable. To an inventor-researcher like Forrest, nobody could be more interesting than Thomas Edison, the greatest living inventor, who would amass 1,093 patents during his lifetime. At the end of the day Edison invited Forrest to come to the laboratory the next morning to meet Firestone and Ford. It was the first of many meetings at Edison's estate, a beautiful maze of horticulture now known as Edison Park. During Forrest's visits there he exchanged opinions and philosophies with the great man. Edison put failure in its proper perspective when he said, "Spilt milk doesn't interest me. I have spilt lots of it. It is quickly forgotten, and I turn again to the future." Forrest's philosophy was somewhat different: "I always want to know all the ways a project *can't* be done. Each failure brings success all the nearer." Edison encouraged Forrest to continue his nutritional research, and the young doctor felt that his vacation was well spent indeed.

The stock market crash of 1929, however, meant that suddenly the Shaklees were no longer financially secure. It was uncertain how long the family could live on savings unless

Forrest opened a practice. Nevertheless, they decided to move to Eugene, Oregon, where the rich fertile soil would yield high-quality vegetables and herbs for Forrest's research.

By the end of a year the Shaklees were unhappy living in Eugene. The almost constant rain and mist were depressing; they decided to relocate again. Forrest remembered one particularly beautiful city they had traveled through in Northern California, a city with a lake in its center: Oakland. On Independence Day 1931 the Shaklees arrived in the city that would become their permanent family home. In nearby Walnut Creek they bought a house set on seventeen acres of land and surrounded by orchards. When they were settled, Forrest opened another Shaklee Clinic, this time in the Ray Building on Broadway in Oakland. Patterned after his other successful operations, it quickly became a busy, lucrative practice.

In his work at the clinic, Forrest continued to be primarily interested in providing patients with proper nutrition, but the urban environment created new problems for him. Mostly he was concerned about the quality of the produce for sale in the Oakland markets. Everything was harvested while it was still unripe, before it had a chance to develop its full nutritional value; the glow on the shiny apples, pears, and cucumbers was the result of wax coatings. Forrest also wondered about the effect of the insecticides regularly sprayed in the fields. Modern technology was moving further and further away from nature. Again, Forrest made a concentrated effort to provide his patients with adequate food supplements. Forrest, Jr., and Lee, now in their teens, continued to help in the clinic, filling capsules in the evenings.

In spite of the Depression, the 1930s were good years for the Shaklees. The clinic prospered and the boys grew strong and healthy. Forrest furthered the crusade for good nutrition by lecturing to capacity crowds on the subject. He also advanced his education, gaining two more degrees, professor of chiropractic and doctor of naturopathy. In 1935 he taught biochemistry at the California Chiropractic College. The boys were equally busy. Forrest, Jr., studied biochemistry and accounting at the University of California in nearby Berkeley; Lee later attended the same school and developed an interest in radio technology.

During the summer of 1941, tragedy struck the family when Ruth Shaklee was run over by a car while crossing the street in downtown Oakland. Critically injured, she lingered on for several agonizing months, only to pass away just before the attack on Pearl Harbor. A month later Lee enlisted in the navy, and shortly after that Forrest, Jr., joined the army. Following the war, Forrest, Jr., worked in radio and public relations, and then opened his own accounting firm. Lee entered the insurance field, where he worked his way up to an executive position.

Less than two years after Ruth died, Forrest decided to retire from his practice. He was financially well off and he felt the desire to try something new. He purchased an isolated 420-acre ranch outside Willits, California, two and a half hours north of San Francisco. On the land he constructed ponds for wild fowl and a wooden lodge, as well as two cabins.

Although he had retired from active practice, Forrest could not leave his vocation as healer behind; when patients tracked him down he worked with them. When others demanded their vitalized minerals, he began compounding the capsules again. During this time he was glad to see a growing public awareness of the part nutrition plays in good health. One sign of this awareness occurred during the war, when the United States government issued its first report on recommended daily allowances of vitamins and minerals.

While he continued to work as a chiropractor and nutritionist with people who sought him out, Forrest was increasingly interested during this time in the influence of the mind on an individual's health and well-being. In 1945 he sold the ranch and began writing a series of articles on this subject. Two years later he founded the Shaklee Foundation and had the name of his philosophy, "Thoughtsmanship," copyrighted.

Thoughtsmanship incorporated some of the ideas of Edison, Macfadden, Hubbard, and even Professor Santinelli; and it rested on Forrest's lifelong belief in the power of Nature. As President of the Shaklee Foundation, Forrest spent much of his time on the lecture circuit; public speaking became almost second nature to him. In 1951 four volumes on Thoughtsmanship were published: *Thoughtsmanship for Well Being, Thoughtsmanship in Love and Marriage, Thoughtsmanship for the Bride,* and *Thoughtsmanship for the Salesman.* The Commonwealth University in Los Angeles awarded him a doctorate in philosophy for these works.

By this time Forrest's name was known through much of Northern California, since his popular lectures were now broadcast by radio stations in San Francisco and Oakland. The response to his talks was so great that he had once again begun producing food supplements. He was continually worried, however, that retail outlets would provide a poor means to distribute his product. Since slow turnover might result in a loss of effectiveness, he searched for another means of distribution.

In the fall of 1955 he asked Forrest, Jr., and Lee to meet with him. He told them about the products, and talked about the growing public interest in nutrition. He talked about his own preoccupation with research on protein, which was obviously of vital importance in maintaining health. He also told them that he believed his products must be distributed through personal contact with the consumer.

"Are you guys halfway interested in starting a business with me?" he concluded.

Forrest, Jr., and Lee had grown up nourished both by food supplements and by their father's philosophy. It wasn't long before they pledged their support of the idea. Then the work of structuring the business began. In the months to come they agreed that person-to-person selling was the best way to guarantee contact with each customer. They also agreed that Forrest Shaklee's philosophy, with its emphasis on the interrelationship between nature and health, must be incorporated in the business. On April 1, 1956, six months from the time the three men first met to discuss Forrest's idea, the Shaklee Corporation opened its doors.

For all their faith in the Shaklee product and philosophy, the three partners could not be certain the new company would succeed. Just as Forrest Shaklee had only his knowledge as collateral when he set up his first practice in 1915, their assets consisted primarily of their accumulated knowledge and their belief in what they were doing. Nevertheless, they felt confident.

For Forrest Shaklee, the new company was a chance to use everything he had learned over the years. Obviously, his knowledge as a nutritionist and research scientist would be of fundamental importance, since Shaklee could only succeed if its products were sound. His contributions would range far beyond research and development, however. His dynamic speeches at sales meetings would attract and motivate new salespeople. His ability to work with individuals, refined over decades of one-to-one contact with patients, would serve as a basis for the company's person-to-person sales approach. His studies of theology would lead him to formulate a company policy of fair play which would build a unique loyalty in the Shaklee sales force. His philosophy, Thoughtsmanship, would influence Shaklee people to live more positive, successful lives. Finally, his characteristic inventiveness would contribute to the unique structure of the Shaklee sales organization.

To the new company, Dr. Forrest Shaklee brought the knowledge and skills he had gained in a lifetime of diverse activity. All of his creativity and learning now focused on a single purpose. His greatest achievement was yet to come.

2

〜〜〜

The Early Years

TODAY, a quarter of a century after Shaklee was founded, it's obvious that starting the company was a brilliant idea. However, as the business adage goes, "Great ideas are a dime a dozen, but the men who have the ability to implement them are priceless."

Dr. Shaklee's great idea was to cost $18,000 initially. Forrest, Jr., closed his accounting firm and Lee resigned from the insurance company. The $6,000 each son invested represented his life savings. They both knew that beginning a food supplement company would be a risky venture at best. In 1956, only determined athletes jogged or ran, and a breakfast of cold cereal and white toast was considered a healthy meal. Few people were concerned about the nutritional content of the food they ate. The American public believed itself to be the best-fed nation in the world—ever. The buying public wasn't anxiously waiting for Dr. Shaklee's nutrients. Almost every potential consumer would have to be educated before he would become a customer.

Lee explains, "Back in 1956 even those consumers who did know how important nutrition is probably didn't know how to evaluate their personal needs."

The most important thing for the consumer to realize is that "everyone is his own supply sergeant," says Lee. "Only the individual can take care of his own body's need for nutrition. If he fails to do this, he's shortchanging himself. Once you put this message across, the consumer convinces himself." Good health, Lee would tell the salespeople, is like an insurance policy; and it's likely to be the least expensive insurance the consumer will ever buy.

Out of economic necessity the partners decided to start their business by introducing only one product. Pro-Lecin was Dr. Shaklee's choice; it combined protein and lecithin, a substance found in the framework of all cells. If people took only one food supplement, he believed, it should be Pro-Lecin.

Distribution of this groundbreaking product would be the Shaklees' most difficult and challenging problem. They were certain of one thing. They would not be able to reach the consumer through the supermarkets or drugstores. "We would have to pre-sell the consumer with a major advertising campaign," Lee explains, "and the cost was simply prohibitive." Even if they were able to place Pro-Lecin in the outlets without supporting the distribution with expensive advertising, the turnover would be so slow that the freshness of the product could not be assured.

There were other problems with supermarket distribution. Pro-Lecin would be lost in the store. There were no sections devoted to food supplements. And one couldn't expect a store clerk to answer questions about the unusual product, or to give advice.

Other means of distribution were carefully considered. Mail order was unsatisfactory, since, again, consumer awareness would have to be created through extensive advertising. To go a step further and teach consumers how to determine their individual needs would be impossible without personal contact.

The Shaklees finally agreed that a direct sales organization would be the most effective means of distribution. The start-up costs of such a business could be kept to a minimum, with very little advertising necessary. At the same time, it was an ideal vehicle for education. "The more we discussed it," Forrest, Jr., explains, "the more certain we were that it was necessary to talk to the customer on a one-to-one basis." Said the father to his sons, "We'll teach some and they'll teach others." As the sales structure evolved, the Shaklees adopted a motto: "Teach others to teach others to teach others." Not only would the necessary knowledge be passed on this way, but so would the enthusiasm of the three Shaklees.

It was then decided that the sales organization should be made up of independent distributors rather than a salaried sales force. To make such an organization work, they knew that they must put together a highly motivated sales team— ambitious people who were sold on Shaklee. At that point they made up their minds that the only way to attract the entrepreneurial types that they wanted was to offer them a compensation plan with unlimited earning potential. Many companies promise sales recruits that their income will be limited only by their own ability and ambition, but very few deliver. Once salespersons are drawn into the arrangement they find out that there are territorial restrictions, escalating quotas, and de-escalating commission rates. The Shaklees agreed that this would never happen to the people who joined them. They would have the most highly motivated sales group in the world. "We will give them the greatest earning potential ever," Lee said.

Lee, who was experienced in sales management, was in charge of marketing and promotion. Forrest, with his background in finance, became the business manager. Dr. Shaklee, of course, was responsible for product development and was unofficial general manager. Each had complete respect for the capabilities of the others, and there was never any conflict about areas of responsibility. If asked about a bookkeeping procedure, Dr. Shaklee would respond, "You'll have to check with Forrest about that. He knows that end of the business better than I do." Forrest, likewise, had no hesitation in referring a question about sales to Lee. For his part, Lee notes that he "could concentrate entirely on sales and marketing. I had zero concern about product development, or about the bank accounts and business affairs. I knew my father and brother were handling those things, and I didn't have to give them a second thought."

Their mutual trust was based not only on respect for one another's abilities but on the knowledge that each had a deep commitment to the business. All three worked long, hard hours. As the business grew, the partners became more involved in their individual responsibilities, and often went their own ways for a week or more at a time without seeing one another. They were able to do this because, as Lee says, "We *knew* we were all working hard. In the beginning there were areas where our work overlapped. But usually we worked separately. I never worried about whether Dad and Forrest were pulling their load; I knew they were."

Overhead had to be kept to a minimum when the company was launched. The Shaklees rented desk space and part of a storage room in an office on Fourteenth Street in downtown Oakland. Since all three were often out in the field, especially during the first year, they used the part-time services of a receptionist who took phone messages and typed some correspondence. A single filing cabinet held all the company's sales materials and records. The company didn't have any expenses in financing its salespeople, the Distributors purchased only what they needed to fill their orders.

All three knew that Shaklee's success or failure was dependent upon the quality of its products. They had pledged that unless a product was the finest of its kind on the marketplace, it would not be introduced. They also knew the entire company had to be sales-oriented. "We were all too familiar with companies that didn't support their sales forces," Lee explains. "No company survives just by manufacturing products. Everybody within an organization has to be sales-oriented."

The Shaklees used to say, "If we're all going to eat, somebody's got to be out there selling." Every new employee was told that the emphasis in Shaklee was on the direct selling of fine products. Distributors were taught how to present the products, and then how to service and follow up the sale. "Selling implies considerably more than selling a product, taking the money and running," Lee would emphasize. "That's just the beginning. What we stress at Shaklee is the importance of providing service *after* the initial sale."

The first Shaklee salespersons were recruited through an ad in the *Oakland Tribune*. Two people responded. One was Luke Thomas, who had previously worked in direct sales with his wife, Florence. They agreed to invite five other couples to attend a meeting. Dr. Shaklee's presentation was so enthusiastic and convincing that Luke and four others signed Distributor applications that evening. The following day the sixth came to the office and also signed up. Luke Thomas, who became the first Distributor, represented Shaklee until his retirement.

As the sales force grew, Forrest and Lee often spent their spare time in the field making calls. They tried house-to-house selling, knocking on doors to see how Shaklee products would be received. They soon discovered, however, that the products sold best through referrals. Forrest explains that gaining referrals became an art in itself. "We might ask a customer if she'd noticed any difference since she began using the products. Often she'd say, 'Well, yes, my friend was saying, "Gosh, you have so much energy lately, what have you been doing?"'

"So then we'd ask for the name of the friend, and that person would almost certainly become a customer, because she was pre-sold. So we trained our people how to ask for referrals and to be alert to any opportunities like that."

Distributors found that Pro-Lecin sold best when they met with the consumers on a monthly basis. Often a Distributor found when he came to take the next order that the customer had several referrals and that these people—or maybe the

customer himself—were also interested in joining the Shaklee
family.

The basic Sales Plan, masterminded by Lee, was formulated by the time the company opened its doors. Numerous
small adjustments and refinements over the years have re-
sulted in an incredibly successful direct selling enterprise with
a formula every salesperson has dreamed about.

Having worked in sales for years, Lee was well acquainted
with the weaknesses that plague most sales organizations. His
first concern was to try to eliminate those deficiencies. "With
our Sales Plan," he explains, "it's not possible to sell too much
and therefore receive a commission cut—and that does happen with most companies. We also have no territorial limita-
tions, so it's impossible to have your territory cut or changed.
You don't have to worry about being undercut by an envious
sales manager, since he or she benefits by your success. And
it's not possible in Shaklee to recruit or train too well, so that
somebody gets taken away from you after you've developed
him. If you're a Sales Leader (a Shaklee field person in a mana-
gerial position), your salesperson isn't going to be promoted
away from you, so that you're left with an open territory to
develop again. In short, we made it impossible to do *too good*
a job."

A vital feature of the plan was incentive—the series of
"carrots" that motivate the individual to reach for new goals.
In formulating the Shaklee Sales Plan, Lee considered the
exact size of the incentives, the distance between them, and
the sequence. For the ambitious Distributor, these incentives
provide a series of distinct achievable goals to pursue. (Chapter
3 gives a description of the Sales Plan.)

Most Distributorships are husband-wife teams. Shaklee's
family orientation begins right at the top. Lee refers to Claire
as "the greatest asset I ever had. No matter where I went,
she went with me. At meetings she related very well to the
other women, and often when we talked to couples it was
the wife who would become a Distributor first, thanks to

Claire. I think the fact that she worked side by side with me gave us a lot of credibility. We were always talking about Shaklee being a family effort, and she demonstrated that was true."

Forrest and Lee drew less income out of the business during the first few years than they had earned at their former jobs; for the company to grow, profits had to be reinvested. Yet neither Claire nor Forrest's wife, Glenda, ever complained or lost faith. Forrest reminisces about coming home and "bouncing ideas off Glenda. She was a great sounding board, whether I needed to talk about a problem or about something I had accomplished that day."

Dorothy Potter, Dr. Shaklee's fiancée, was involved in the business from its inception, although it wasn't until fifteen months later that the couple were married. All three women have been so involved with the company from the beginning that their business and personal lives are inseparable. Claire says, "I feel that I gave birth to five children—Rick, *Shaklee Products*, Sandie, Laura, and Karen."

The expansion of the company meant longer hours and more travel than the Shaklees had anticipated. They expected that the company's operation would be limited to the Bay Area of California, which includes Oakland and San Francisco. But the business quickly expanded into Southern California, and the partners found they had to be on the road training and recruiting much of the time.

Although each man had an internal area of responsibility, these meetings had top priority, for the only way to spread the Shaklee enthusiasm was to do it in person. A loose system evolved whereby the Shaklees rotated areas, so that meetings with each area's Distributors were conducted by Dr. Shaklee, Forrest, and Lee at different times. Forrest explains that "although we shared the same philosophies, each of us had his own way of presenting things. Sometimes one person would come across where another one didn't. It's like this in college, where a student can repeat a course with a different professor and get a whole new slant on the same subject. Suddenly it comes easy! We figured that if we exposed our sales force to all three Shaklees, surely each individual would relate to *one* of us!" After the first year, business had grown so much that the three Shaklees were seldom able to appear together except at company-wide conventions.

To have a Shaklee conduct a sales meeting was a special event, but people who remember the old days say that the *real* meeting began when the meeting was over. Because so many people drove considerable distances to meetings in those days, the Shaklees always ended the meetings promptly. Lee would announce, "Anyone who has to leave now, go right ahead. As for me, I'm going to stay to answer questions, however many questions you have. I'm going to stay till the last dog is hung!"

The questions from new Distributors often flew fast and furious. Lee remembers that in meetings held in public places, "the janitor would often come in at two in the morning and ask us to leave so he could clean up. Staying so late was tiring, but it was great, because it got across the message that we were there to help. You could see how much people appreciated that extra time." Afterward, Lee often talked on with the salesperson who had arranged the meeting, sometimes going out for coffee and a sandwich. "It wasn't unusual for me to get to bed at four in the morning," he remembers.

Forrest remembers the Shaklee distribution system of the early years—"my Plymouth station wagon! I'd put the back seat down and load the floor with products. Then Glenda and I would drive down to Fresno for a meeting with maybe twenty to forty people. After the meeting I'd sell the local Supervisor whatever was needed for the next week, and then we'd drive down to Modesto with Flora Hardin (now Flora True) and have a midnight snack. Glenda and I would get home just before dawn. And you know what? I loved it."

At those early meetings it was already clear that the people attracted to Shaklee's products and philosophy were not ordinary salespeople. In fact, at one early meeting, when Dr. Shaklee had invited a professional speaker to address the group, the speaker asked him, "Do you want me to tell you what I really think about your salespeople here tonight?"

"Yes," Dr. Shaklee replied.

"Well, to be honest with you, you don't have a salesman in the whole lot out there."

"I suppose you're right," the doctor said calmly. "But they sure do sell a lot of my products."

Early Distributors had an uphill battle, for aside from those who knew of the former Shaklee Clinic in Oakland, few people recognized the name Shaklee. The name itself was a disadvantage for Forrest, Jr., and Lee when they went knocking on doors or conducted small living-room meetings. "There might be four or five people there," Forrest says, "and here I am showing them a product with my name on the label! They had to be thinking, It must be a small company if one of the owners is standing here selling the stuff! Of course, once our name became known, our presence became an advantage, because people felt they were getting the information straight from the horse's mouth.

"It was tough in those days," Forrest affirms. "Today it's much easier because we have a track record. People tend to resist joining a small company. They want you to prove yourself first. We had to persuade an awful lot of doubting Thomases. Pioneering is plain hard work." Forrest remembers those times now when his barbershop quartet sings, "These will be the good old days twenty years from now."

While Forrest thinks of the early days as "pioneering," Lee likes to use the word "crusading." "A crusader picks up his lance and charges onward, no matter what. He has to have a strong faith. When he's knocked down he picks himself up and goes forward again. I don't believe an entrepreneur can survive unless he has the crusader's drive."

Drive and perseverance were needed to survive the long work days the three men put in during the early years. Often they worked sixteen hours a day, six or seven days a week. Instead of lessening as the business grew, the work load became heavier. Forrest worked nights processing orders and Distributors' statements. Lee sometimes stayed up half the night pecking away at his typewriter to prepare a newsletter, type it on a stencil, run it through their mimeograph machine, collate, and staple it.

Although Dr. Shaklee was very much in demand for sales meetings, he continued his research into nutrition. Soon Herb-Lax, an herbal laxative, was added to the product line. In 1956 Liqui-Lea, a vitamin and mineral supplement in liquid form, was introduced; Vita-Lea, a vitamin and mineral supplement in tablet form, was introduced the following year. The sales force kept requesting new products, but nothing left Dr. Shaklee's immaculate laboratory until he was convinced it had been perfected.

Lee compares the efforts of the early days to rolling a hoop. "To get that hoop rolling, you've got to beat on it very hard with a stick. Finally, after a tremendous effort, you get it to stand up and to start bouncing along. Once it's rolling, it's easier to keep it rolling. But you still have to run alongside it and keep your eye on it and whack it from time to time."

The analogy is apt; while starting a new business takes tremendous effort, and may be the most difficult part, every business needs continuing good management if it is to survive. Growth always brings new problems, which can only be solved through trial and error. As Lee says, "You never have it made; you have to keep right on running with it."

The Shaklee hoop came nearest to toppling in 1958, but thanks to the loyal efforts of Flora True, disaster was averted. Flora had joined Shaklee in June 1956, when the company was only two months old. Hearing Dr. Shaklee speak at a sales meeting, she was impressed by the fact that "he never talked about money, but only about how much good we could do for our fellow man." Flora, who had been in direct sales since 1937, was then working for a 70 percent commission. But Dr. Shaklee's speech convinced her that Pro-Lecin was superior to the protein product she was selling and that her earning potential would soon be unlimited. She then agreed to go to work for a 35 to 40 percent commission.

Flora quickly became the infant company's star salesperson. Within two months she was a Supervisor; after six months her sales volume was $3,000 a month—nearly half the company's total! In December 1957, Flora was awarded the first Shaklee bonus car at a dinner in her honor, called "Flora's Hard-Earned Night." For the event she wore a bright red dress. Because of the dress and her constant "scratching away for business," Dr. Shaklee nicknamed her the "Little Red Hen."

The following year a Southern California competitor made a bold attempt to raid the neophyte company, offering substantially higher commission rates to the most successful Shaklee Distributors. At first it seemed the scheme would work; several influential Distributors made the switch, including the man who had sponsored Flora. He had taken others in the Stockton and Santa Rosa area with him, and tried hard to convince Flora to come along.

The Little Red Hen, however, not only refused to budge, but personally called on every Shaklee Distributor in the area to remind them that Shaklee had superior products—and integrity. Had she not done so, the raid might have snowballed, creating a major setback for the company. As Lee states, "It might have put us out of commission; we'd have had to start building the sales organization all over again. It could have been that bad!"

"The Little Red Hen really went out and scratched gravel for us," Lee says, "and she will always have a very warm spot in our hearts." In fact, she's kind of a celebrity. When she calls at the home office, people stop whatever they're doing to talk to her. "She's retired now," Lee reports, "but to this day if someone asks me who was the most important Distributor we ever had, I'd immediately answer, 'Flora True.' "

Despite the attempted raid, by the end of 1958 the original six Distributors had grown to about a thousand. Larger offices were needed for the expanding operations. The company relocated to 1610 Harrison Street in Oakland, and shortly thereafter to Twelfth and Harrison.

In 1962 Shaklee moved into larger quarters once again, at 2035 National Road in Hayward. The same year, the company incorporated. By 1965 there were 13,000 Distributors, and the company had to double its square footage at the Hayward plant; now 20,000 square feet served the company that had started out with a rented desk. Five years later the plant was expanded to 70,000 square feet to serve the more than 50,000 Distributors who now represented Shaklee. In 1974 the company made yet another move, basing its corporate headquarters in the Shaklee Towers in Emeryville on San Francisco Bay.

While products were gradually added to the line, the most significant addition—and the best story—probably occurred in 1960. That year Everett Parsons, a Supervisor in Southern California, called Dr. Shaklee to talk about the competition. "They're selling a multipurpose cleaning product with a lot of success. It would be a good idea for us to have something like that. Might help expand the sales force, and it would be an excellent door opener."

"Let me think about it," Dr. Shaklee replied. As he hung up the phone, his thoughts were already focused on a formula he had tucked away. The formula was the result of serendipity. Some time back, while manufacturing a cosmetic product, he had stopped to work on the stubborn gears of the machine. Afterward he found his greasy hands coated with the oily cosmetic product. When he put his hands in water, they washed perfectly clean. Intrigued by the possibilities of developing a cleaning product from this incident, he had noted the formula of the substance; later he began to experiment with it.

When he talked to Forrest and Lee about the possible cleaning product, they were enthusiastic.

"It may need more work, though," he told them.

"Send Ev a sample anyway," Lee urged when Dr. Shaklee admitted that his tests already showed the product was everything it ought to be.

Less than forty-eight hours after his conversation with Dr. Shaklee, Ev Parsons received two small vials of blue liquid. Ev took the vials to a sales meeting in Garden Grove, where he let the women do a comparison test of the blue liquid with the competitor's multipurpose cleaner. The new Shaklee product won hands down.

Ev made another emergency call. "How soon can we have some inventory?"

"Inventory?" Dr. Shaklee replied. "I sent you all we had!" The next weeks saw a flurry of activity as Forrest procured bottles and caps, Lee sketched out labels and oversaw the printing, and Dr. Shaklee figured out how to put the new cleanser into production. A month later Shaklee was selling what would be one of its most popular products: Basic-H.

In introducing Basic-H, Shaklee was once again breaking new ground. As the company had been a leader in its focus on food supplements, it was now among the first American corporations to produce a biodegradable household cleanser. The philosophy of harmony with Nature led Dr. Shaklee to anticipate the needs of Americans in the decades to come. When the public became aware of the importance of nutrition, Shaklee food supplements were already established and available. Likewise, Shaklee's biodegradable Basic-H had already gathered a loyal following by the time most Americans became aware of the need for environmentally safe products. Undoubtedly, one major reason for the company's success has been this ability to anticipate not just what consumers want but what they need.

Dr. Shaklee's perfectionistic approach to research has paid off handsomely for Shaklee in many ways. Certainly Shaklee would never have gained its present reputation if the products had not worked well for their consumers. Inspired by his own belief in the quality of Shaklee products, Lee suggested that Shaklee should offer an unequivocal guaranteed refund to any dissatisfied customers. Perhaps it was a chancy move, but the Shaklees agreed that if the products weren't good enough to take that chance they didn't deserve to be called Shaklee. The decision turned out to be a good one. Over the years, less than one-tenth of 1 percent of all products sold have been returned for refunds.

In March 1973, Shaklee Corporation took another important step by going public. On August 2, 1977, the company was listed on the New York Stock Exchange. Certainly, being publicly owned adds to any company's credibility, since the preliminary investigations are long and exhaustive. The Shaklees also felt that in making this move they could establish better connections with outside business interests, such as banks and suppliers. Dr. Shaklee "welcomed the idea of having our stock listed on the open market for everyone to purchase and participate in." Forrest concurred, adding that going public "gave everyone a chance to participate in the future, particularly the guy out there in the field." In the same vein, Lee believed it was important to "give the sales force the opportunity, if they choose, to become part of the corporation."

When Shaklee became a NYSE company only twenty-one years after its inception, the event marked a coming of age. A relatively young business, Shaklee joined the elite ranks of the few companies to have ever achieved this distinction so quickly. Shaklee was now generally recognized as the major direct selling company in the food supplement field.

The need for balanced nutrition was becoming apparent in the mid-1950s as American food was being more and more highly processed, with the resulting loss of nutritional value. Shaklee's growth went hand in hand with America's discovery of dietary supplements. Shaklee recognized a void in the marketplace and filled it. The timing was perfect. Shaklee was an idea whose time had come.

Yet, even the Shaklees did not anticipate the phenomenal growth of their company. The 1956 sales volume of $100,000 had become almost $500 million just twenty-five years later. Analysts predict that Shaklee will be a billion-dollar company before the end of the '80s.

Although the three founders are no longer active in day-to-day management of the company, the family spirit and philosophy of doing business lives on. The Shaklee family may have spread throughout the world, but it's still a close-knit family.

3

The World's Greatest Sales Organization

WHEN GARY SHANSBY visits Wall Street to meet with a roomful of securities analysts, he's always asked about the assets of the company.

"They start talking about balance sheets," Shaklee's youthful, energetic Chief Executive Officer says, "and I immediately start talking about our field people. The sales organization doesn't appear on a balance sheet, but it's the number one asset of this company. There's no doubt about it; we've got the world's greatest sales organization."

It is also one of the world's largest sales organizations. Hundreds of thousands of Distributors and Sales Leaders represent Shaklee throughout the United States, Canada, the United Kingdom, and Japan. The people come from all walks of life, but they have at least one thing in common: they all have unlimited opportunity within the organization. Shaklee has broken down the barriers to success. Anyone, regardless of education, work experience, social status, financial background, age, sex, or race, can rise to the very top of the Shaklee sales organization.

Shaklee's dynamic Vice President of Sales, Jack Wilder,

says, "The most important asset you can have in this business is the right attitude. If you have that, you're simply going to make it. If you don't have the skills, we'll teach them to you. This is not a technical business—and isn't it true of successful people in any field that what they have most in common is attitude? After all, our attitudes dictate what our actions are going to be, our actions will form our habits, our habits dictate our destinies. So, with the right attitude it's simply a matter of doing what has to be done again and again."

A new Distributor is "sponsored" into Shaklee by any member of the sales organization. While some direct sales companies require new recruits to make a substantial purchase, the Shaklee person makes only a modest payment for a Distributor's kit. The kit contains a manual outlining everything a beginner needs to know: instructions on how to enter the business; selling or "sharing" guidelines (Shaklee people share rather than sell); and product information. Necessary business forms and literature on nutrition are also included in the kit. New Distributors are told that they get much more than written information when they are sponsored into the company; they get automatic membership in the huge, supportive Shaklee family.

The term "family" is often used at Shaklee to describe the warmth and mutual caring new Distributors receive from Sales Leaders and the people at the home office. "The Shaklee philosophy of sharing is not a matter of idle words," Jack Wilder says. "Everybody is treated as an individual here. Shaklee really does care."

To many new Distributors, the warmth of the Shaklee sales organization is symbolized by Jack, who spends most of his time in the field addressing Shaklee meetings and talking to countless salespeople on a one-to-one basis. Jack's personal warmth and charisma exemplify the enthusiasm and conviction that make Shaklee run. The ex-college athlete, at six foot six tall, towers over almost any gathering, but he intimidates no one. "He's got a heart as big as he is tall. He's the kind of guy you can't resist giving a great big bear hug to," said one Distributor.

The Shaklee Sales Plan is a uniquely structured program of advancement and incentives* and is largely responsible for the astonishing growth of the company. It offers an opportunity for any ambitious person to form a business with no capital investment. In the best spirit of free enterprise, the sales program rewards every individual strictly on his or her performance—and the sky's the limit!

A Shaklee Distributor is often a husband-wife team; frequently the wife joins first and is most active in the business while her husband works full time at other employment. Distributors usually stay at their existing jobs until the Shaklee income provides a comfortable degree of financial security. At this ground-floor level, a Distributor usually purchases Shaklee products from his Sales Leader at a wholesale price, called "Distributors' net." If he then sells to his customers at Shaklee's suggested retail price, there is a 35 percent spread between the two prices. That's the Distributor's basic profit. In addition, he receives monthly cash bonuses of 3 to 8 percent, depending on his purchase volume (PV). He also receives bonuses on the purchases of any Distributors who are sponsored by him.

When a Distributor's volume reaches $1,000 a month, he becomes an Assistant Supervisor, and his bonus rate increases to 11 to 14 percent, again depending on the volume. In addition to selling, he now supervises his Distributors, becomes their supplier for Shaklee products, and conducts sales meetings to educate and motivate them.

The next level of promotion is Supervisor, which requires monthly purchases of at least $3,000. Now the monthly cash bonus leaps to 22 percent plus 1 percent for cash purchases. And a Supervisor is eligible for insurance, company-paid trips, and bonus cars—again, all depending on his purchase volume.

---

* A comprehensive explanation and a diagram of the sales structure are given in the Appendix.

When four of his Distributors become Supervisors, he is promoted to the position of Coordinator, and he becomes eligible for a generous retirement plan. But there is still room for advancement. The Coordinator will become a Key Coordinator when nine or more of his Distributors have become Supervisors. And, finally, he becomes a Master Coordinator when fifteen or more of his people become Supervisors. At this level, annual earnings often run into six figures. (Six profiles of a cross section of Master Coordinators are included in Chapters 5 through 10.)

Although there are six levels in the Shaklee sales structure, the total cost of the bonuses is less than the markup on a product sold through a typical retail outlet. This is true because the "middleman's profit" from manufacturer to wholesaler to jobber to retailer is eliminated by direct selling. Also, Shaklee does not advertise its products; and the cost of advertising is a major factor in the price of brand-name retail products.

Although the Shaklee sales organization is multilevel, this structure should not be confused with the illegal "pyramid" structure. Pyramid sales companies became infamous in the 1960s when many people lost large sums of money by investing in them. In a typical pyramid organization, A sells B the right to be a distributor. If the distributorship sells for $10,000, A keeps, say, $5,000 and the company receives $5,000. B then sells C a distributorship for $10,000, and A and B keep $3,000 each while the company's cut is $4,000. In this process money is made by selling the right to sell—not by selling products. As long as more "investors" can be recruited in an unending chain, it doesn't matter whether anyone ever sells a product or not. In the end someone has to be a big loser.

In a multilevel company such as Shaklee, on the other hand, no one buys the right to sell. Profit is realized only when products are sold to the consumer; a Shaklee person does not earn one cent by simply sponsoring someone new into the company. Positions aren't bought or sold—nothing influences advancement except performance—and the requirements for advancement are well defined. A salesperson doesn't have to wait for his superior to quit, be promoted, get fired, transfer, or retire. What's more, there are no territorial or product line restrictions.

Lee explains that in Shaklee "there's no place for the get-rich-quick individual. Shaklee people must care. They must want to give. It's a slow, steady building process—and what they build is solid."

Not everyone who becomes a Shaklee Distributor gets rich, but thousands have, and many thousands earn more money than they ever before dreamed possible. What about the others? Some get into the business without any intention of building a real Distributorship. They are Shaklee customers who love their products and "sign on" to supply themselves, their family, and friends; and are now able to buy at a favorable discount. Some others don't want to put out the effort necessary to make a success of it and eventually become inactive. But getting back to those who really take their Distributorships seriously, to them Shaklee is Aladdin's lamp, the fairy godmother, and their lucky star all rolled into one. Lots of the successful ones start out expecting only to supplement their regular incomes with a little extra money, then get caught up in the business.

As Shaklee grows, so does the number of high-level salespeople who attend its annual conventions. Nearly 2,800 Sales Leaders attended the 1981 International Coordinators Convention (ICC) in San Francisco, where they celebrated the company's twenty-fifth anniversary.

Everyone receives red carpet treatment at a convention. Qualifying Sales Leaders are flown to the conventions, lodged in the finest hotels, dined in the best restaurants, and royally entertained between meetings. Master Coordinators get a "little extra" in honor of their achievement: deluxe hotel suites and chauffeur-driven limousines for the duration of their stay.

Past conventions have been held in some of the world's most glamorous cities, including Acapulco, Honolulu, New Orleans, London, and Vienna. Throughout the five-day 1981 ICC, the Shaklee Players, a group of professional actors and actresses, entertained with a program especially written for the appreciative audience. San Francisco's new and beautiful Davies Symphony Hall served as the location for several of the general sessions, while smaller meetings were held at the convention hotels.

Sales Leaders are encouraged to bring their children to conventions, and can earn all-expense-paid trips for their entire families. For the children, a lavish youth program is provided. At the 1981 ICC, the attractions included trips to Chinatown, Marine World, the Cable Car Museum, and Alcatraz. Many of the children help in their parents' businesses, and already have plans to be the Sales Leaders of the future.

While the youngsters play, the adults are deeply involved in business meetings. They deal with nutrition, new products, selling techniques, new company services, and other related topics. Speeches are delivered by Master Coordinators and high-ranking company executives. Applause often interrupts these talks; no outside speaker could appeal to this audience the way a member of the family does. At general sessions the achievements of top Sales Leaders are recognized by their induction into the President's Club.

After the ICC, hotel managers commented that Shaklee conventioneers "sure aren't typical." They stay up late not to drink but to exchange ideas. Many of them feel that the informal discussions that go on in individual hotel rooms long after the evening meetings adjourn are the best learning experience of all. And although meetings start early in the morning and activities are scheduled until late at night, it's rare to see anyone dragging his feet, even by the end of the week. As one conventioneer said, "If your blood doesn't run fast in your veins at the ICC, then you don't have blood in your veins!"

The convention inspiration is not left behind in the meeting halls; many a Master Coordinator testifies to the impact an earlier Shaklee convention had on his or her career: "I sat out there and listened, and said to myself, 'I'll be a Master like him next year.' Then I went home and went to work—and here I am!" The message to new Sales Leaders is clear: "I did it, and you can do it too." For most Sales Leaders, conventions are not just a time of reunion and learning and fun but also a time to set goals for the year ahead.

The goals are often big ones, but this is not surprising; today everything is done in a big way at the conventions. In 1981 Shaklee held the largest sit-down banquet not just in the history of Shaklee but in the history of San Francisco. Over 2,800 people attended the formal dinner. No restaurant could accommodate the huge crowd, so an abandoned pier was converted for the occasion. Portraits of the guests served as place cards, and the silver-plated wine glasses the guests drank from were given to them as souvenirs.

Each of these conventions is marked by something special that adds a warm, human touch to the huge event. Several months before the Silver Jubilee, the company requested that all of the invited salespeople complete and return cards answering the question "What do you wish for?" The card went on to say that it's fun to dream, and to ask for your fondest wish: "It doesn't matter what it is, but think of the wish that means the most to you."

On the first day of the convention everyone found out what the card was all about. Jack Wilder announced that three of the wishes would come true, compliments of Shaklee. One wish would be granted each day.

The first wish was easy to fulfill, but meant a great deal to the recipients. It was wished that a man and wife could spend some time with Dr. Shaklee, whom they had never met. At one time the founder of the company knew every Shaklee Distributor. Today, of course, that's impossible. There are hundreds of thousands of Distributors, so for many of the newcomers to the company the elderly gentleman (now in his eighties) is something of a legendary character. ("I don't know what all the fuss is about," Dr. Shaklee has been heard to say. "I appreciate the expressions of love, but people shouldn't make a hero out of me. All I ever did was listen to Nature and pass the word along.") Of course, the meeting was arranged.

The second-day winners were a woman who had been born in Calcutta and her husband. They wished that a supply of Shaklee food supplements be sent to Mother Teresa, 1979 recipient of the Nobel Peace Prize. Not only was the wish granted, but Shaklee arranged for the couple to go to India so they could personally present the gift to Mother Teresa.

The third wish to come true was that of a young couple who had incurred unexpected heavy medical expenses when their seven-year-old daughter was stricken with a serious illness. They were handed a check for $10,000.

This program was, of course, much more than just part of the evening's entertainment. It was symbolic of the message Shaklee continuously sends out to its Distributors: Wishes and dreams can come true; good things do happen to Shaklee people.

Shaklee grew to a half-billion-dollar corporation because its top management is committed to its products; and because its members are absolute masters at motivating their sales organization. They don't harass the people who sell their products. They don't threaten them with expulsion, demotion, or relocation. They gently coax them into producing, with attention, financial incentives, and expensive rewards. They don't dangle carrots that are just out of reach. The money and the rewards are attainable, as thousands of their Distributors can attest to.

It's not unusual for a salaried salesperson to drive a company car, but it's almost unheard of for an independent contractor to be given an automobile by his supplier. But what is practically unheard of in the selling industry has become commonplace in Shaklee's operation. Automobiles are an example. Don't get the idea that the cars are simply giveaways, because they're not. They're earned. Not everyone who sells Shaklee products receives one. But they're available to everyone. Right now more than 5,000 salespeople drive them, and that number grows every year. And these are not stripped down bottom-of-the-line models. They range from Chevrolets to Cadillacs and Continentals—to even a Rolls-Royce. The cars are earned the same way promotions are earned—strictly on sales volume. There's no politics involved; the incentive program is carefully and clearly laid out. Each person knows exactly how far he has to stretch to grab the carrot. That's the way it is with every facet of the Shaklee Sales Plan.

Lee and Forrest Shaklee dreamed up the idea of making bonus cars available to the salespeople. They would have given away homes if they could, but that seemed impossible. Who knows? Maybe in the future.

Lee recalls, "In 1957 we presented the first bonus cars. Five of them! Boy were we excited." The Shaklees were just as excited when they hosted their first company-sponsored convention in 1962. It was a two-day affair. The group included office, plant, and sales people and their families, 110 people in all.

"The entertainment," Forrest remembers, "was a bus ride from Oakland to our plant in Hayward. We gave them a two-to-three-hour tour of the place and refreshed them with punch and Shaklee's Instant Protein. That convention cost us two thousand dollars—our 1981 Coordinators Convention cost three million!"

Several one-day conventions are held regularly in each country where Shaklee operates. These events, called "jubilees" and "rallies," are as spectacular as the International Coordinators Convention. They are likely to be attended by Gary Shansby, Jack Wilder, or other high-ranking home-office executives. Jubilees and rallies are regional and open to all Shaklee Distributors and Sales Leaders; as a result, attendance is often as high as 10,000 people.

Jack Wilder says that although Shaklee's top Sales Leaders

have very different styles and approaches to the business, they have one thing in common. They hold a *lot* of meetings. There, the successful people tell about their methods and express their attitudes, and those positive attitudes are contagious. Novice Distributors in particular need to hear again and again about the successes others have enjoyed. "We never underestimate the power of pep talks." Just as important as the large gatherings are the small weekly meetings.

Every Shaklee meeting large and small lays stress on motivation, recognition, and education. The salesperson's conviction—his desire to share—is of prime importance. "Selling is really nothing more than a transfer of feelings from one person to another," Jack says. "If you feel enthusiastic, that will come across louder than words. A Distributor can say, 'John, I'm not very good at this, and I'll level with you, I'm not the greatest nutrition expert in the world. But I feel so good about Shaklee products that I'd like to share them with you.' If you believe that and can say it with enough conviction, your customer is likely to go along with you. You certainly don't want to try to come across like the world's foremost authority on the subject of nutrition.

"Anybody can succeed in this business," Jack adds. "So often when I speak, somebody from the audience will approach me to say, 'But I've never sold anything. I'm not sure I can do it.' Then the next time I see those people they're bubbling over with their success in Shaklee. They say, 'I can't believe how my life has changed and how many lives I've changed!' "

Many Distributors who become Sales Leaders never dreamed they would make it. "Their job now," Jack Wilder says, "is to obtain, train, and retain." The new Supervisor learns how to share with people, how to educate and motivate new Distributors, and how to keep his group active.

A high percentage of successful Supervisors are former housewives, Jack states. "It's incredible how many housewives enter the job market for the first time with Shaklee and become star performers. Most of them have never before had an opportunity to develop into business people. They might first come to Shaklee as consumers, but their conviction and enthusiasm carry them right to the top! Understanding and caring for people is what counts, and in Shaklee we really educate them. They get their master's degree in people."

If somebody comes up with a good idea that works, he's expected to tell others about it. "We're a copying business," Jack says. "We try to make it so there's nothing that *can't* be copied in training new people. But I don't call it *copy*ing. As they say, 'If you steal an idea from one person, it's plagiarism, but if you steal from two or more people, it's research.' I tell our people to research the heck out of everything and then adapt it to their own style."

While the learning process may be informal in the beginning, many go on to become quite knowledgeable on the subject of nutrition. The company holds two-day seminars throughout the United States that serve as excellent cram courses in nutrition. For home study, training presentations are available on cassette tapes, and Sales Leaders can obtain video tapes from the home office to use in group presentations.

Shaklee not only wants to make its products available to anyone, but also its business opportunities. Because the United States has a large Spanish-speaking population, most sales materials are now available in Spanish. Shaklee has special equipment to aid blind and deaf Distributors. The deaf can communicate with the home office via teletype, and training materials are available on tape cassettes for the blind. Also, many Shaklee products have the kosher seal of approval.

Thousands of Shaklee people have used "In Harmony with Nature," a cassette coordinated with a training script, which teaches a Distributor how to present Shaklee on a one-to-one basis. The salesperson who studies this course learns how many of the U.S. Recommended Daily Allowance of nutrients (RDA) are contained in the typical American diet, how stress affects nutritional needs, how supplementation works, and much more. The individual has a better understanding of the short-comings in his own diet, and of which Shaklee products can best serve him. Shaklee people are cautioned, however, not to prescribe. "Instead, they educate," Jack Wilder says. "They point out the need for supplements."

Jack is constantly in the field, spending more than thirty weekends a year on the road. The five regional sales managers who report to him cover the entire United States. They conduct meetings in their territories and act as liaison between the field and the home office. "Unless we know what's going on in the field," Jack says, "we can't be effective at the home office. Good communication is one of the strongest things we've got going for us, and that's the way it has to be."

Another source of feedback from the field is the network of Master Coordinators who head large Distributorships within the Shaklee world. Although each is an independent contractor running his own business, he or she is in constant contact with the home office. When you look at the total picture you see that Shaklee really is thousands of businesses—large and small, with their own chief executive officers—that add up to one of the world's largest distribution systems. Also one of the largest communication systems.

One way Gary Shansby and Jack Wilder keep in touch with the Masters is through the Executive Committee of the Masters' Advisory Board. This committee meets quarterly and is composed of six Masters elected to work with the home office on products, convention planning, bonuses, company services to the field, and on Privileges and Responsibilities, a guideline on procedures for Distributors and Sales Leaders. The committee frequently suggests changes and new ideas to the home office.

The home office consults with lower ranks of field people as well as Masters before introducing new products. It asks their opinion on consumer appeal and on how the product can best be sold. New products are compared to the competition's in field tests by small "focus groups." The reports of these groups give the company unprejudiced feedback on how the Shaklee product compares with other brands. Field people are also consulted each year through an in-depth questionnaire administered by an independent survey company. Shaklee is concerned about the opinion of everyone within the sales organization—from the experienced Masters to the Distributors who have just received their kits.

As Lee Shaklee told a group of Master Coordinators, "Don't ever forget that you are where you are because of the sales your Distributors make. If you ever forget their contributions to your success, you'll lose them. And Masters aren't the only people who should keep that in mind. Every single person at the home office needs to remember it, too." In the same vein, Gary Shansby comments, "I hope that even when we're doing five billion in sales we keep our humility and remember where we came from."

Shaklee prides itself on its communications with the field. It has simplified ordering by installing elaborate computerized telephone systems. A Sales Leader calls in an order and within minutes receives confirmation of the products' availability, cost, and shipping date. The home office handles all inquiries from Sales Leaders through a computerized switchboard called "automatic call distribution." These calls are placed with counselors who have been trained to answer questions on just about everything one needs to know about Shaklee. The counselors on this hot line are trained to project the Shaklee family relationship.

Shaklee publishes three magazines, *Reporter, Shaklee News,* and *Survey.* These monthlies cover the latest company news and include articles on nutrition and health, how-to and self-help information, profiles of successful Sales Leaders, and recognition for special achievements. In addition, virtually every Master publishes a newsletter that is circulated to his sales organization.

What kind of person is most likely to become a Distributor? Home-office personnel assert that it is impossible to typecast the Shaklee person. The company includes professional and business people, retired people, housewives, the disabled, factory workers—you name them, Shaklee has them. Personality types vary greatly as well. Since Shaklee encourages low-pressure selling, many introverts have become "superstars" in the Shaklee organization.

People become Shaklee Distributors for a wide variety of reasons. As Jack expresses it, "Some people come into this business because they're attracted to the potential earnings, while others simply want to buy the products and share them with their friends and family. Everybody starts out with the same investment of $12.50, but how many times that investment is earned back depends entirely on the individual salesperson. For those who are willing to pay the price of success, Shaklee gives one of the few opportunities to *earn while you learn.* You get out of this business what you put into it, and it's a very easy business if you work hard at it. It's up to the individual to decide for himself how much he wants to achieve. But big or small, everyone in our sales organization is an important person to us."

Distributors and Sales Leaders claim that Shaklee makes a change for the better in their lives. Many husband-wife teams testify that working together deepens their relationship as they learn to complement each other's strong and weak points. They also believe that their families are happier since joining Shaklee. Not only are their children healthier but they are often involved in the business, so they can have a sense of contribution. "That's one important reason why we invite kids to our conventions," Jack says. "This is a family business in every sense of the word."

Furthermore, when a new Distributor becomes interested in good health and harmony with Nature, the whole family benefits from it. Ask any Shaklee person and you will hear that Shaklee is not just a job, it's a way of life. As Gary Shansby says, "If you're drinking excessively, smoking, and overweight, you can't go out and sell health and fitness. It just won't fly!

Shaklee has been described as an automatic self-improvement program, and you know, that's not bad."

Jack Wilder perhaps sums up the feelings of the Shaklee people interviewed for this book when he tells his own thoughts about his job. "We're not selling ordinary products— a cake of soap or pots and pans," he explains. "We're sharing a product that makes people feel better. What's more, we offer our people a better standard of life. A recent survey indicates that the biggest fear the average American has today is that his standard of living will decrease. Many families have incomes they once thought would be more than adequate, but with inflation they can't make ends meet. So they've been forced to reduce their dreams to fit their incomes. But with Shaklee, people can raise their incomes to match their dreams."

Jack takes a moment to reflect, and adds, "I suppose the greatest thing about my job is that when I retire I'll be able to look back at all the people I've helped have a better life. That's what makes this business so great for all of us. You have to help people to be truly successful yourself, and this is a 'people helping people' business."

At a recent convention Gary was seated in the audience with a securities analyst from New York who said, "Tell me about your sales force. What kind of people are they?"

"Turn around and look at the people in the audience," Gary replied. "Study them for about thirty seconds, and then tell me what you see."

The analyst turned to look at the enthusiastic people filling the huge auditorium—a cross section of people representing a wide diversity of ages and ethnic backgrounds who had come from all over the United States, Canada, the United Kingdom, and Japan. Slowly he turned back and said to Gary, "I've never seen such happy people in all my life."

"They have a lot to be happy about," Gary said. "They're the leaders of the world's greatest sales organization."

Dr. Shaklee as a young man

Dr. Shaklee. As a young chiropractor he
grew a mustache and beard to look older.

SHAKLEE'S

VITALIZED
MINERALS
A concentration
of Nature's Values

SHAKLEE'S HEALTH
LABORATORIES

Dr. Shaklee's original product,
pre–Shaklee Corporation

Dr. Shaklee and Dorothy Shaklee

World War II—Forrest, Jr.,
Dr. Shaklee, and Lee

Dr. Shaklee at work

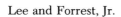

Lee and Forrest, Jr.

The company's second office,
at 1610 Harrison in Oakland

Gary Shansby and Dr. Shaklee

Lee, Dr. Shaklee, and Forrest, Jr

CHAPTER

4

❦

Shaklee International

SHAKLEE MADE a commitment to international expansion in 1973, shortly after the company became publicly owned. A year of planning went into the project. Although the long-range plans were very ambitious, the first decision would limit the overseas market potential. Shaklee would take its products only to those countries that allowed and nurtured the free enterprise system. And too, management agreed, they would operate only where direct selling was permitted and practical.

Their next decision proved to be a near disaster. They would launch their international program in ten foreign markets—*simultaneously.* So, before the end of 1974, they set up in Canada, the United Kingdom, Ireland, France, the Benelux countries, and Japan. They knew that developing an efficient worldwide distribution system would be difficult, but they weren't prepared for the nightmarish quagmire of red tape, legal roadblocks, and logistical problems that plagued them.

Each country had its own rules and regulations regarding vitamins and food supplements, and they sometimes varied dramatically from those of the United States. In some countries, vitamins and nutrients are classified as drugs and can be obtained only with a doctor's prescription. Some ingredients that have been accepted as beneficial and safe in the United States are still illegal in some other countries, and a number of the Shaklee products would have to be reformulated to meet the specific criteria of their new markets.

They expected problems—language barriers, currency differences, and shipping difficulties—but the regulatory and legal issues almost brought down their expansion program before it had a chance to get off the ground. The company was pouring money into the project but was making little headway.

In 1976, a year after he joined the company, Gary Shansby became Shaklee's Chief Executive Officer; he immediately went overseas to try to untangle the situation. It didn't take long for him to know that "we moved too far too fast." He acted swiftly. "In a single day—telephoning from a hotel room in London—we cancelled all of our activities in Germany, France, Ireland, and the Benelux. At the same time the decision was made to put our efforts into developing the Canadian, U.K., and Japanese markets."

Canada and the U.K. were obvious choices: a common language and a similar culture, background, and value system. Also, the logistics of "doing business" were less complicated than in most other places. But Japan, to many, seemed the least likely candidate for overseas expansion. On the downside were the distance, the language barrier, and what at first seemed to be a distinctly foreign culture and lifestyle. On the plus side were the fervent Japanese belief in the free enterprise system, the passionate respect the people have for good health and their bodies, and the neighborly relationship that exists among the people.

Another positive though less obvious factor was soon apparent: Dr. Shaklee's unshakable conviction that man must live in harmony with nature was absolutely in tune with the philosophy and religions prevalent in Japan. To Gary Shansby, the positives far outweighed the negatives, and the company was committed to building an important Far East subsidiary.

Allan Nagle heads up Shaklee International. A Harvard business school graduate, he had held senior executive positions with Gillette and Brown & Williamson and was well prepared to handle the complexities of an overseas organization. He needed a product line that would not only meet the legal requirements of each government but also appeal to the populace of each country. He needed an active sales organization, and that meant designing a sales plan that would motivate the Distributors and enlighten the consumer about nutrition. And he needed an efficient, effective vehicle to move Shaklee products around the world, a distribution system that would get the goods out quickly as well as assuring that the products were fresh and of the highest quality when they passed into the hands of the user.

It seemed that Britain would be the easiest of the foreign markets to develop, but it wasn't. Somehow the program didn't catch on. The first people to become Distributors sold the products all right, but they didn't develop sales organizations. They held on to their customers but didn't convert them into new Distributors. After four years the program floundered, and it appeared that Shaklee had completely misread the English market. But in 1978 Jimmy Jensen, who had been general managing director for Pillsbury in England, joined Shaklee and that was the turning point.

The Hegermans—Al and Joan—agreed to leave their lucrative business in Minnesota to spend a year in England helping Jensen build the sales organization. And they were successful. The Hegermans became the friends and mentors of Barbara and Bryan Jacques, a young couple who sold Shaklee products to their friends but didn't recruit Distributors. The Hegermans were good teachers and the Jacqueses fast learners, and in less than three years Bryan and Barbara became Great Britain's first Master Coordinators. They had heard some of Shaklee's U.S. success stories. The stories seemed too good to be true; but when the Hegermans came to England, the Jacqueses not only saw that the stories were true but they became convinced that they could do it too. "There's no magic to it," Bryan says. "Al and Joan proved that to us. Just a willingness to work and a complete belief in the products and the program."

The Canadian operation was put into motion a few months before Gary Shansby's reorganization of Shaklee International. Steve Locke, still in his twenties, was hired as managing director. He knew direct sales, having worked for Avon and Fuller Brush, and was enthusiastic and optimistic; however, the introduction of Shaklee to the north was anything but auspicious. Steve was a victim of International's early entanglements. In order to comply with Canada's criteria for nutrients, many of the products had to be reformulated, and the plant set up to do the work was in Ireland. Unfortunately for Steve, that plant hadn't ironed out all its kinks, and the products he needed weren't coming through quickly enough in the quantities he needed. He spent months developing his Sales Plan, producing selling material, recruiting Distributors, and trying to keep his recruits in place until the products began flowing in. All this time he worked in his home—his kitchen table was his desk.

When Gary Shansby closed down the plant in Ireland, the production of Canadian products was shifted to the U.S. By the time the new sources could assure Steve of a steady and reliable supply, he had laid the groundwork for a solid operation. Then he received an unexpected boost. Master Coordinators Madeleine and Roger Trottier decided to put together a Shaklee sales organization in their native Canada. They had started their career in California in 1967, and in five years had built a thriving business to become the twelfth Master Coordinators in the U.S. Two years later they moved their base to Florida, where they went into partnership with their daughter and son-in-law, Nicole and Robert Alo. For a while the Trottiers split their time between the two countries, spending a few months a year in Canada recruiting Distributors and building a solid sales base. In 1980 they made their move to Quebec, and it was a move not without some risks. They turned over their share of the Trottier-Alo partnership to their children, and in so doing gave up the prestige and income of Master Coordinators. But they were pros. They knew the business well, and entered into their new venture with the same enthusiasm and confidence that had carried them to the top several years before. It took them five years to reach the level of Master Coordinator the first time. This time they did it in quick time—only thirteen months. Thanks to them and Irene and Bertrand Dufour, the first couple to achieve that rank in Canada, thousands of Shaklee Distributors have proven the viability of the Canadian subsidiary.

The growth and development of the British and Canadian subsidiaries are truly success stories, but what happened in Japan is nothing short of remarkable. In 1981, only five years after Shaklee entered that market, Japanese sales topped $100 million! It had taken Shaklee U.S. seventeen years to reach that figure.

The president of Shaklee's wholly owned Japanese corporation is Masaaki Matsushita, a former Fulbright scholar who was educated at the University of Virginia and Bennington College, as well as the University of Hokkaido in Japan. Mr. Matsushita,* who speaks fluent English, has an impressive business background, which includes serving as managing director for the huge American trading company Muller and Phipps, and heading the Japanese operations of International Playtex. Mr. Matsushita is credited with the company's phenomenal success. In fact, according to some experts, it is the single greatest success story in the history of direct selling anywhere in the world.

The Shaklee opportunity came to Japan at a time when many Japanese were searching for a solution to a widespread social problem—early retirement. In Japanese companies, re-

---

* While first names are used elsewhere in this book, all Japanese people are referred to by their surnames, out of respect for the Japanese custom of addressing only family members and very close friends by their first names.

tirement is frequently mandatory at age fifty-five or sixty. Since pensions tend to be very small, retirees can face many years of relative poverty. They are also beset by the chronic problems of old age—poor health, inactivity, and loneliness. For these people, Shaklee offered a way to maintain their health, make money, and find friends. It is not surprising that many Japanese Distributors and Sales Leaders see Shaklee as a lifeline, and honor the company that has given them an opportunity to solve these problems and build more meaningful lives.

Another factor in Shaklee's success is the position of women in Japan. While Japanese women have definitely emerged from their historically subservient role, they are still far behind American women in attaining liberation. Shaklee offers a Japanese woman a rare opportunity to achieve something on her own. Interestingly, a Japanese woman is more likely to continue to run her business alone, even after achieving considerable success. American men often become intrigued and attracted to Shaklee when their wives' businesses reach a certain size, but Japanese men tend to have a deep commitment to a permanent employer-employee relationship and are therefore less likely to leave their jobs and join their wives in Shaklee.

Nevertheless, the success story of a typical Japanese woman is often touchingly similar to the story of her American counterpart. Mrs. Shinozaki, for example, was suffering from a familiar problem, the empty-nest syndrome. With her three children grown and gone, and no skills but those of a housewife, she was left with time on her hands and a feeling of worthlessness.

Mrs. Shinozaki's self-esteem was low in late 1976 when she heard that Shaklee was now operating in Japan. Her daughter, who had married a Pan American pilot and settled in San Francisco, told Mrs. Shinozaki about Shaklee. Immediately she signed up for a Distributorship. A shy, introverted woman, she shared Shaklee with her friends and neighbors in a low-key and indirect way; but she worked hard at her new career. Ten months later she qualified to become a Supervisor. Mrs. Shinozaki was so shy that the prospect of speaking at sales meetings terrified her. Her friends offered to conduct her meetings if she would hold them, and for some time her sales meetings proceeded in that way.

By October 1980, Mrs. Shinozaki had become a Coordinator. A year later she made Key Coordinator. From a recluse she has changed to an active, happy woman who can speak in front of large audiences. She heads a large organization and enjoys an income that puts her in the top percentile of the Japanese population. Her financial independence is a great joy to her; but perhaps most meaningful to Mrs. Shinozaki is that her children respect and admire her as a capable, independent woman.

Not only did Mrs. Shinozaki help herself but she is especially grateful that she's been able to help others. When her niece was widowed and left with four young children to support, Mrs. Shinozaki traveled ten hours by train to teach her about Shaklee. Today the young woman is a Shaklee Coordinator, enjoying financial independence and security.

Based on her own experience, Mrs. Shinozaki firmly believes that "Shaklee happiness is contagious."

Shaklee people in Japan identify both with the Shaklee philosophy and with Dr. Shaklee as a man. Rather than seeing Shaklee as an impersonal institution, the Japanese tend to see it personified in Dr. Shaklee and his philosophy. The respect for him sometimes approaches adulation.

As in the U.S., Canada, and the U.K., bonus cars and conventions are offered as incentives. However, because of the availability of good public transportation and a general lack of parking space, many people do not drive. As a result, more than one Sales Leader has declined a bonus car. Nevertheless, the car is still a significant status symbol. The story goes that one Japanese Coordinator proudly accepted her bonus car and has never driven it. It sits parked in front of her house,

washed and polished, a tangible sign of her achievement and
an incentive for her Sales Leaders.

Not all Japanese are motivated by bonus cars, but all appreciate the Shaklee convention program. Great lovers of international travel, the Japanese work hard to qualify for conventions. New Supervisors come to visit the company's
headquarters in San Francisco. All who qualify attend the annual International Coordinators Convention. The Japanese
hosted the International Achievers Convention in Tokyo in
August 1982.

The Shaklee people in Japan are terrifically proud of their
company's achievement. But they also take great pleasure
in and celebrate the achievements of the individuals in the
organization. It is of particular delight to them that one of
Japan's most famous and beloved entertainers is an active
Shaklee Supervisor. He is Yukio Hashi. The only singer in
Japan ever to be twice given the Grand Prix award (as best
singer of the year), he has had a successful career for over
twenty years and has starred in thirty-six films. Just as Mr.
Hashi has shared his belief in Shaklee with friends in the entertainment world, he has shared his talent with Shaklee friends
at conventions. At the 1980 National Sales Leader Convention
he entertained, then he delivered a talk about Shaklee that
left the audience virtually hypnotized.

Foreign conventions (each country usually holds about four
a year) are attended by at least one executive from the home
office. These trips help bolster the daily communication between San Francisco and the home-office operations in each
foreign market. Allan Nagle averages two trips a year to each
subsidiary. Both Dr. Scala, Vice President of Science and Technology, and David Lough, Vice President of International Development and Administration, make one or two trips a year
to each subsidiary. Gary Shansby, Shaklee's CEO, travels at
least once a year to each country.

All foreign markets are serviced by the International Science and Technology Group, which has its headquarters at

the Forrest C. Shaklee Research Center in Hayward, California. This group oversees special manufacturing and quality-control procedures necessary to service each country. The products (often reformulated) may be made at the Norman, Oklahoma, plant and shipped in bulk to Canada, Great Britain, or Japan for packaging; or they may be manufactured by wholly owned subsidiary companies; or sometimes they are subcontracted to manufacturers in the foreign countries. "Because we buy in such great quantities," says Ron Bailey, who heads International Science and Technology, "the economics dictate that we purchase many of the raw materials here and ship them out in bulk to our foreign subsidiaries. Then, too, there are a few items which we don't use in the United States that we nevertheless buy here and keep in inventory as a service to our foreign operations." Whatever the method of manufacture and packaging, International Science and Technology sets and monitors quality-control standards to insure the products are uniformly fresh and of high quality.

International is a fast-growing segment of the company, accounting in 1981 for approximately 20 percent (about $100 million) of the company's total sales volume. Because of the company's success with its international operations, plans are presently being made for future expansion into other foreign markets.

Shaklee's success can be attributed to the validity of the business and personal philosophy of its founder, Dr. Forrest Shaklee. He believed that personal values can be compatible with good business practices. Shaklee International has demonstrated that his beliefs hold true throughout the free world.

CHAPTER

5

The Best Investment Ever Made
(*The Hegerman Story*)

YOU DON'T HAVE TO SEE the Hegermans' income tax returns
to know that they have attained the American Dream. Today
they enjoy all the trimmings of success. Their beautiful contemporary home includes five bedrooms, six baths, a large
indoor pool, and a sauna. "His" and "Her" Cadillacs are nested
in their attached garage. Their spacious living room displays
dozens of decorative mugs, all collected on the many trips
abroad they have taken with their children. And, to escape
the frigid Minneapolis winters, the family also owns a three-
bedroom condominium on Coronado Shores in San Diego.

But they didn't always enjoy the good life. Al had been
selling pots and pans for the two years since his high school
graduation when he and Joan met in 1949. After they were
married the following year, he went to work for Electrolux
and sold vacuum cleaners for several years. Then he sold
Fuller brushes and Singer sewing machines for a brief time.
Joan had her hands full raising their children, but she too
gave sales a try, and claims to have failed miserably. "I was
a resounding flop as an Avon Lady. When I quit after a few
months, I had earned only enough money to pay our tithe
to the church, with an extra hundred dollars left over for
us."

In 1958 Al decided to pursue his lifelong ambition to become a policeman. Not only did he make a clean break from
selling, but the family moved to San Diego, California, where
Al joined the police department. The couple were content
living on his salary, and it wasn't until four years later that
they ever heard about Shaklee.

Two "sisters" (a devout Mormon, Joan refers to other
women of the church as sisters) came to visit the young mother
after her fourth child was born. One of the women, a Shaklee
Distributor, handed her a bottle of Basic-H, and during the
lulls in the conversation about the new baby and what was
happening at the church, she talked to Joan about her Shaklee
career. In passing, she mentioned the ways Joan could use
the cleaning product to make her housework easier. Joan paid
little attention to the instructions, and gave no further thought
to the Shaklee opportunity.

In November 1962 the family decided to move back home
to Minneapolis, where Al would again be a policeman. Just
before the move Joan happened to run into the woman who
had given her the Basic-H. When her friend asked how she
liked the product, Joan confessed that she only used it for a
few things. Then and there the Distributor gave Joan a full
explanation of the many applications of Basic-H. "I had no
idea there were so many ways to use it!" Joan exclaimed.
"For heaven's sake, why didn't you tell me all of this before?"

"You never asked." The Distributor shrugged. Then, sens-
ing Joan's interest in the product, she said, "Say, why don't
you become a Distributor?"

"I had no intentions of actually selling anything," Joan explains, "but I signed up because I wanted to be able to buy
the Basic-H at Distributor's cost. I was busy getting ready
for the move and it was a quick way to get rid of her. I thought
that if I bought it for myself and a few friends, that would
be plenty. So I bought two quart bottles to take back home
to Minneapolis."

As Joan points out now, she had several strikes against

her when she became a Distributor. "I didn't know how to drive a car," she explains, "and I couldn't walk very far. We were about to move to an area where I hardly knew a soul. And I was going to peddle a cleanser."

After the Hegermans moved, Joan began using the Basic-H on everything in her house. She was so impressed with the results that she started talking about it to her new neighbors and they wanted some too. She generated enough enthusiasm in them that she ordered a case from her San Diego sponsor. Joan succeeded in exciting her neighbors about the product to such an extent that they ran out to greet the truck. But the freight cost on the case was $7.35. "When I finally sold all the bottles," she recalls with a sigh, "I had made only $7.32. So I ended up with a net loss of three cents!"

The driver was so impressed that he too bought two bottles. As a bonus, he explained to Joan that she could have three cases shipped for the same freight charge as a single case. "I'm no mathematical genius," she says, "but it didn't take me long to realize I'd make more money that way." With three cases coming the next time, Joan was even more motivated to spread her enthusiasm about Basic-H. Getting the money for those three cases from Al was, she says, "my biggest sale in my whole life."

Joan's motivation was doubled by an impending crisis. Shortly after the family arrived in Minneapolis in 1962, she learned she would have to have surgery on her hips. She had been born with both hips out of their sockets, and had corrective surgery at the age of two. But now the hip bones were wearing through into the nerves. The doctor told her she would not be able to do any housework for a year after the operation. On a policeman's salary, the Hegermans could not possibly afford a housekeeper. Joan's Shaklee career had to be a success.

Joan worked hard, but selling bottles of Basic-H was not highly lucrative, since she netted only sixty-one cents a bottle. Periodically Al would ask her, "Why are you fiddling around with that crazy soap?" Joan asked Al to sell Basic-H, but he said it was a nickel-and-dime business. If he had to, he would rather go out selling vacuum cleaners or insurance.

"I didn't quite understand why I was doing it," Joan says now. "I just knew that something within me was saying, 'This is the answer to your prayers. Keep going, kid!' "

Meanwhile, Joan took advantage of every conceivable opportunity. She talked about Shaklee at church, in the store, to cab drivers. Whenever a repairman came out—for the plumbing, gas, or refrigerator—Joan gave him her presentation about Basic-H.

For some reason during all this time, Joan had never received a Sales Manual. Finally she decided to write Lee Shaklee with some questions about the company. Lee wrote her a long letter and sent her a Sales Manual and other Shaklee literature.

When the manual came, Joan gave it to Al to figure out. By the time he finished reading it, he was so excited he was shaking. He said to Joan, "If this opportunity is what it says in this book, this is the greatest opportunity on earth!" Suddenly the Hegermans had become a Shaklee team.

Al's enthusiasm was so great that when he went to pay the rent he asked the landlord, "How would you like to make a million dollars with me?"

The landlord responded sarcastically: "What bank are we gonna stick up?"

Then Al told him about Shaklee. When Al came home that afternoon, he told Joan, "I guess you'd better hurry up and sponsor me, because I've just sponsored my first Distributor."

As their Shaklee income began building, the Hegermans decided to buy a house and applied for an FHA loan. They were turned down, on the grounds that a second income was not counted until the loan applicant had been in the business for two years. The Hegermans bought the house with conventional financing. But more important, being turned down for the FHA loan made them think about their future and do some goal-setting. Two years was a good period of time; they would "have some fun for the next two years and see what happens to our Shaklee business," Al explains. "Then we'd decide whether we wanted to stay in it any longer."

From the moment he read the Sales Manual, Al was convinced that the greatest opportunity with Shaklee existed in sales management, and he set their goal. They would build a sales organization. In November 1962 Joan became a Distributor. In May 1963, seven months after becoming a Distributor, Joan sponsored her brother, a door-to-door salesman, who happened to call at the house, and a nurse she met in the hospital. In June, just before Joan entered the hospital, she and Al called on all their retail customers and sponsored twelve couples. By the end of June the couple had twenty-five Distributors and placed an order for $3,600 worth of Basic-H.

In August 1963, when Joan went in for the first of numerous operations, the Hegermans had already become Supervisors. If possible, Joan's enthusiasm for Shaklee had grown. After eight hours on the operating table, she woke up. Forced to do without further anesthetic while the operation was completed, she talked on and on about Shaklee. She sold Basic-H to everyone in the operating room.

For weeks she lay wrapped in a plaster cast from shoulder to toe, with only her arms and one leg free. She asked Al to bring her a case of Basic-H—what else?—for her to lean the good leg against. In no time, she sold that case and had Al bring in three more, one for the good leg and two more to sell. People from all over the hospital came in to talk to "the spot lady" about the problems they had cleaning their uniforms.

With Joan's attitude, the Hegermans were soon making more money than they had ever made in their lives. Far from feeling sorry for herself—Joan would walk with a limp from now on—she said, "Thank God for Shaklee. You know, when you've got people to be worried about and work with, you forget about yourself."

Soon after Joan recovered from her first operation, the Hegermans qualified for their first bonus car, a new Chevrolet. When the car arrived at the dealership in Fargo, North Dakota, Al decided he couldn't wait for it to be shipped. He took a Greyhound bus up to Fargo to pick it up.

"I was so excited," he says, "that after I looked at the car I asked the dealer, 'Well, what do I do now?'

"He looked at me and said, 'Well, I suppose you get in, turn the key, and drive it out of here.' "

The Hegermans have since had ten bonus cars: two Chevrolets, seven Cadillacs, and a Mercedes. They have just ordered their 1983 Cadillac Fleetwood Diesel. Al, the family mathematician (Joan says, "When I add, the columns seem to move"), figures that in eighteen years the Hegermans have had $118,000 worth of cars; and they have not made a car payment since 1963. Incidentally, the first Cadillac delighted Joan so much that she made a monumental personal decision: she would learn to drive. "I wasn't going to let Al have that car for himself," she says gleefully.

The Hegermans' early success, selling only Basic-H, was unprecedented. When Al wrote asking to attend a California sales meeting, Lee wrote back, "You don't have to come out here. Dr. Shaklee and Dorothy want to go out there to see you." In November 1963 they came. Dr. Shaklee was impressed with the Hegermans' success, but he also wanted to know *how* they were doing it.

At that time, Basic-H accounted for about 11 percent of Shaklee's volume. Yet, while most of Shaklee's sales were in food supplements, the Hegermans' personal group was selling between $4,000 and $5,000 a month worth of Basic-H, and nothing else.

"I'll never forget our first meeting with Dr. Shaklee," Joan says. "When he got off the plane he didn't say, 'Hello,' or mention how cold it was. He just stuck out his hand and said, 'What's wrong with the rest of my products?' "

In preparation for the visit, Joan and Al had rented the East Room at the Curtis Hotel and "practically begged" everyone they knew to come. Eighty-three people showed up and, as Al comments, "many of the people we sponsored that night are still with us today."

Luckily for the Hegermans, Everett Parsons, a Distributor from California who had been vacationing nearby, attended the meeting. He had with him a complete display of the company's products. "If it hadn't been for that," Al admits, "we would have felt foolish having only one lonely bottle of Basic-H on display for Dr. Shaklee's visit."

After the meeting—which was an unqualified success—Dr. Shaklee sat until 3:00 A.M. talking to the Hegermans about Shaklee, giving special emphasis to the skin care program. "When we left, we were practically floating," Joan remembers. She immediately began using the skin care products and telling her friends, relatives, and Distributors about them. Within a few months she had begun giving skin care training classes to groups of women. The classes became so popular that as many as 150 women attended.

In the skin care classes the Hegermans worked as a couple. While the women learned skin care, Al conducted meetings with their husbands and boyfriends, explaining the Shaklee Sales Plan. Joan also used the classes to sell other products.

"In every class, when I got to the point where the women would put on masks for twenty minutes," she explains, "I'd tell them, 'Don't talk, because it might crack.' Then I talked about food supplements and how 'what you are inside shows on the outside.' " With this technique, Joan really built up the group's sales of food supplements. Naturally, she herself is a believer. As she comments, "When anyone asks me how much I take, I jokingly say I just take enough till I rattle comfortably."

At least one Cinderella story has taken place in a Hegerman

skin care class. A woman had been engaged for seven years, but she and her fiancé somehow always put off marriage. "She wore such heavy makeup," Joan says, "that you wondered how much would come off if you scraped your fingernail across her cheek." In the class, the woman's face was cleaned and toned. When her fiancé, who attended Al's class, saw her at the end of the evening, he did a double take: "My God, Evelyn, you look ten years younger." And, as Joan recounts triumphantly, "they went out and got married that very night!"

Al never failed to be impressed by Joan's recruiting. "If she'd see a salesman going down the street who looked like he was going to miss our house, she'd send one of the kids down to get him. She'd listen to his whole pitch, and then say, 'Okay, I've listened to you, and now it's your turn to listen to me.'

"I remember one time when we went to Washington the skycaps were sitting around talking about a possible strike. Joan told them that since they might be having some time on their hands, they could sell Shaklee! She never missed an opportunity."

In her informal presentations, Joan begins by selling people on the product, then she tries to sell them on the company. Actually, instead of asking whether they are interested in making some money, she says, "Do you know anybody who'd be interested in becoming a Distributor? We're looking for additional people in this area."

"You see," she explains, "if I ask someone directly if he is interested, he'll say, 'What's the matter, do I look like I'm poor?' But if I put it this way, he'll say, 'Hey, lady, what about me? I'd like to make a little extra!'"

Both Al and Joan enjoyed their first years in business together, but the time came when they had to think seriously about their commitment to Shaklee. Al flew to San Francisco to meet Lee Shaklee and other company people and tour the plant. Upon his return, he and Joan agreed there was too much opportunity in Shaklee to pass up. "Let's go after it!" Al said. The couple sat down, worked out a long-range business plan, and they began to build their organization with a new all-out commitment. They started to build slowly, with "solidarity" in mind. They felt a strong obligation to train and encourage new Distributors and made a concentrated effort to develop top Sales Leaders.

By 1967 the Hegermans were making $50,000 a year in Shaklee. They had a live-in housekeeper, an office, and a secretary. Al was still working on the police force, "as a street cop, not even a sergeant. I was probably the only cop in America earning the kind of money I was making and driving to work in a new Cadillac." Despite his love for police work, the Hegerman organization was growing so fast Al decided to leave the department and devote all his time to his Shaklee career.

When Joan and Al talk enthusiastically about their years in Shaklee, it sounds easy—as if there were never obstacles to overcome. But Joan's limp tells a different story. At the beginning of her career with Shaklee she had surgery on her hip; this was followed by two more major hip operations. In 1972 she had a radical mastectomy and has since suffered a second bout with cancer. All told, the feisty blonde has had twenty operations over the past eighteen years.

Far from keeping Joan from her Shaklee work, the operations inspired her to occupy herself with building the organization. "Thank goodness we're in this business," she says. "Where else could a person work out of a sickbed?" During every convalescence, she occupied herself with making telephone calls, writing letters, and selling and recruiting everyone who walked into her hospital room. "My physician always wondered how I could have such a positive outlook during my illnesses," she comments. "I told him I simply didn't have the *time* to worry." Financial considerations helped motivate her. "I can't even begin to comprehend where we would be financially," she says, "if I had suffered my health setbacks and didn't have Shaklee."

Al nods and quotes his personal philosophy: "With every adversity comes the seed of an equivalent or greater success." Joan's illness meant the Hegermans had to succeed in their Shaklee career; and in turn, her work in Shaklee helped her endure her long, painful convalescences. "Sure, there have been times we've been down," Al admits, "but fortunately, never both of us at the same time. When Joan was down, I pulled her up, and vice versa."

In 1969 the Hegerman organization faced another kind of adversity. The Teamsters went out on strike, which meant no products could be shipped. The Hegermans' Sales Leaders "had every penny in the world tied up in orders of Shaklee products that were just sitting out there in a San Francisco warehouse." Joan and Al knew they would lose the organization they had worked so hard to build up if they didn't do something quickly.

"My daughter and her boyfriend were discussing this with Joan and me," Al relates. "One of us said, 'Why don't we get a whole bunch of people together, fly out there, rent some trucks, and bring the orders back?' And that's exactly what we did."

The Hegermans sent ten men to San Francisco, where they rented a fleet of trucks. Only one member of the caravan, a Teamster on strike, had ever driven a truck before. The trip was not without setbacks. Coming down the Donner Pass, one driver panicked, threw the truck into reverse, and ripped out the transmission. Another driver was arrested because he didn't have the proper license.

Still, the caravan's arrival in Minneapolis was triumphant. Al had called the Sales Leaders telling them to go to the Farmer's Market. An hour after the caravan arrived, every truck was empty. The Hegermans had saved their business.

Newcomers to Shaklee often envy Al and Joan for having entered the business in "the good old days." But, as Joan explains, in the early days things were not quite so easy. "There were no visual aids and no advertising," she points out. "There wasn't even a recommended way to give the Sales Plan.

"It was also harder to sell food supplements back in the early sixties. People didn't want to hear about it. They acted as if we were some kind of health nuts when we talked about supplementing their diets. In those days, most people didn't know the dangers caused by processed foods and the degenerative diseases that result from poor nutrition. Today, people are health-conscious and much more receptive."

Al jokes about the early difficulties they had selling Shaklee products. "Heck, in those days when we talked about Basic-H people confused it with Preparation H. And when we said 'Shaklee,' they thought we made pizza. Their attitude was, 'Well, you go ahead and use those products, and we'll sit back and see what it does for you.' Then, too, when we tried to recruit people into the organization, we didn't have the success stories of other Distributors to talk about the way we do today. And as they say, 'Success breeds success.' "

Al smooths the lapel on his hound's-tooth suit jacket and chuckles. "People say to us now, 'Oh, but you were in on the ground floor.' We weren't—we were in on the *basement.* We were the first Supervisors qualified east of the Rockies. We were absolutely all alone out here—pioneers."

In recent years Joan and Al have spent a major portion of their time speaking at Shaklee functions throughout the United States. Both are excellent speakers. Joan's talk is personal, emotional, and spontaneous; often she deals with the handicaps she has had to overcome during her career. Al's message is business-oriented and focuses on such subjects as the opportunities in Shaklee, recruiting sales techniques, and how to operate a successful Distributorship.

In front of audiences ranging from a handful of people to several thousand, Joan talks freely about her personal problems with a mixture of humor and sincerity that moves the audience to laughter and tears. "I didn't have a limp before I had corrective surgery on my hips," she sometimes says. "That's the practice of medicine—they're still practicing! Naturally, I was very upset when I discovered that I was going to waddle like a duck for the rest of my life.

"I can't help but believe that through the years the Lord has whispered to me, 'It's okay. By being this way you can show others that if you can do it they can too.'

"And you know, I can live with that. I have a friend who is blind, and we have a standing joke between us that when we get to the other side, she's going to watch me run."

When Shaklee had attempted to expand into the United Kingdom, only a small nucleus of a sales force had been established. The company approached the Hegermans and asked if they would be willing to take their family and spend a year in England. Joan and Al sat down with a pencil and paper to try to make an intelligent decision. Al recounts, "The list of reasons why we should go was two pages long, and there were only two reasons why we shouldn't go—our mothers. But they understood.

"Actually, we had three main reasons for going. First, everything we had from a materialistic standpoint we owed to Shaklee, so we felt an obligation to help the company. Second, after fourteen years in the business we were getting a little stale, and we thought a change would do us good. Third, it was a tremendous opportunity for the whole family to discover a different culture for a year."

In October 1976 Joan and Al left for London with their three youngest children. During the next twelve months they worked untiringly to build the United Kingdom sales organization. The company, in return, provided them with deluxe living quarters, a housekeeper, and a Mercedes, and arranged for the children to go to private schools. For the Hegerman family, it was a wonderful, enriching year; they spent a long weekend visiting a different European country every month. For the Shaklee Corporation the year was equally rewarding. The Hegermans' goal had been twenty-five new Sales Leaders at the end of the year, but when they left there were thirty-three. Today there are 120 Sales Leaders in the United Kingdom, and business is thriving. Joan says, "We showed them over there that if a lady with a limp and a bald ex-cop could be successful, anybody could."

At the end of that year the Hegermans experienced perhaps their greatest thrill. They were honored at the International Coordinators Convention in London. As a group, the English Distributors stood and sang a farewell song to the American couple who had changed their lives. And then, in front of several thousand people, including the three youngest Hegerman children, Gary Shansby designated Joan and Al International Masters in recognition of their contribution to the United Kingdom Shaklee organization—for services over and above the call of duty.

The Hegermans' Shaklee earnings have shown steady growth from their first year, when they made just under $6,000. Their yearly earnings now exceed $350,000. Their organization, one of Shaklee's largest, has an estimated 24,000 people. Hegerman Sales Leaders can be found in forty states and Canada, while members of the Hegerman organization are in every state in the country.

Joan and Al are obviously as enthusiastic as ever. They're still working full steam with no plans to retire. If they did, however, their retirement residual bonuses from their Shaklee organization would be well in excess of $150,000 a year— and it all started with that initial purchase of Basic-H.

6

The Greatest Self-Improvement Program in the World (*The Spargur Story*)

IN 1968 Carolyn Craft Spargur was a nervous wreck. Two of her four children were sick. Her marriage was on the verge of collapse. She was unhappy with her job. "A nervous wreck!" she recalls. "Without tranquilizers and sleeping pills I couldn't get from one day to the next!"

Then a woman at work tried to talk Carolyn into joining Shaklee. The timing, it seemed, couldn't have been worse.

As a bookkeeper-secretary to a CPA attorney in Southern California, Carolyn knew she was being underpaid. She was making $500 a month, and practically everyone she knew was making more. Lorraine Mansfield, for instance, was making twice that amount. Carolyn was therefore shocked when Lorraine quit her job "to sell some product door-to-door. She just didn't seem the type."

But Lorraine told Carolyn, "I've found the most exciting business with the most wonderful products—you should get into it." Carolyn was unimpressed. "Selling was one career I had never considered. Besides, I needed to 'get into something' like I needed a hole in the head."

Lorraine gave her a quart of Basic-H and asked her to try it. The bottle went into the back seat of Carolyn's beat-up car, and there it stayed.

Carolyn ruefully remembers those months of trying to make ends meet while the quart of Basic-H rolled around in the car's back seat. Every time it banged against the front seat she would mutter under her breath, "Oh, there's that dumb stuff Lorraine gave me!"

When she ran out of her regular household cleanser, Carolyn finally uncapped the Basic-H. She cleaned all day, then relaxed, sat back, and inspected her hard work. "My old furniture looked new to me, and it even smelled new. Wow! Why does everything look so good? I looked at my hands—I'm allergic to a lot of things—and my hands were fine. Then it dawned on me that this product I was using was terrific!"

Enthusiastically, Carolyn persuaded all her friends to try Basic-H. For the next six months she bought the product retail and resold it to them for the same price. It didn't occur to her that she was "selling" the product to her friends. She had an aversion to salespeople—at least she was turned off by most of those who approached her. Her only attempt at selling had been when she was a child and it was Girl Scout cookie time. "I couldn't bring myself to ask anybody for a dollar to buy some cookies, and conveniently got sick."

Now it struck her, she *was* selling and was pretty good at it. Only she wasn't making any money. By the time she was ready to join Shaklee, Lorraine had left town. However, one of Carolyn's co-workers had become a Distributor and agreed to sponsor her. She was reluctant, however, because the word was out that "Carolyn never sticks with anything, so don't spend too much time with her." Carolyn admits that she was like that—at the time. Until then, she had been a person whose interests were short-lived. She would plunge into a project, then quickly tire of it and quit.

"Shaklee has changed me," she says with a glowing smile. "There's something built into their system that keeps me reaching and keeps me motivated. My work gets more exciting all the time."

The young mother who "never liked selling" had a purchase volume of $5,000 a month by her third month as a Distributor. Until then Carolyn was selling only Shaklee's Basic-H. All she knew about the product was that it was the best she had ever used and she loved it. Her lack of information began to bother her. She decided that if she was going to take her business seriously she needed to know more. She phoned Bob Ewing, a Coordinator in the area, who invited her to a sales meeting scheduled that evening. From there on, her involvement with Shaklee increased and her earning power soared. For the first time she learned about Shaklee's food supplements.

In the next months, Carolyn read everything she could find about nutrition. She began taking Shaklee products herself, supplementing her diet with Instant Protein, as she believed it would help her nervousness. Her divorce was pending and she was now the family breadwinner, yet she kept feeling better and better. Before long she dropped the sleeping pills and tranquilizers.

Carolyn started talking Shaklee everywhere she went— not as a salesperson but as a woman and mother sharing her own experience. Three months after she had become a Distributor, Carolyn climbed to the second level of the sales structure; she became a Supervisor.

She knew that she "was on her way" and put every penny of bonus money into building the Shaklee inventory in her garage. Instead of buying lunch at school, the children took peanut butter sandwiches; Carolyn brown-bagged it too. The pennies saved went into inventory.

Meanwhile Carolyn held on to her office job. Finally she was ready to quit; out of loyalty to her boss, she waited out tax season, when the office work was heavy, and then she resigned. The next year she earned about $12,000, or twice what her salary had been. The year after, she earned $36,000. When her former employer completed her income tax returns, he exclaimed, "This is the lady who used to be my secretary. She now makes more than many attorneys do!"

Although money was important to Carolyn, it was conviction that drove her and made her successful. *"No*body got by me," she says with a wide smile, *"nobody.* I was out to save the world from poor nutrition. My tongue was constantly going. I talked to everyone about our wonderful products. The preacher. The man at the filling station. The Boy Scout leader. The lady down the street. The teenager visiting the next-door neighbor. I didn't exclude anybody.

"And I never felt as though I was *selling* them anything. I had something to *share* with them that I believed in with all my heart and soul."

Carolyn worked hard, even when she herself didn't realize a cent out of it. She remembers once driving from Huntington Park to Riverside, California—about sixty miles each way— just to deliver one bottle of Herb-Lax. "And I did it even though I knew I wouldn't get paid for a month!" she says. "But I did it because that lady loved the product and *she needed it.* I felt I had a mission to perform. And I believe that nobody will last long in this business without that conviction."

Carolyn didn't really understand the Shaklee compensation plan, although it had been explained to her many times. Each time Bob Ewing would review it with her, it still didn't seem to sink in. She'd say, "Bob, I *still* don't understand how it works." Although she might not have understood all the benefits Carolyn received from sponsoring others, she kept bringing in new Distributors. "Whenever I needed a lift I'd sponsor another person," she says, "and that just did wonders for my morale."

Carolyn developed an approach that has remained successful for her to this day. "I always ask new contacts, 'Are you interested in better health and more money?' and they automatically answer yes to both. Then I give them the Sales Plan."

For Carolyn, her first bonus car was a dream come true. "Since then I've had Coupe de Villes, El Dorado convertibles, and a Mark V," she says. "But none of those cars thrilled me quite like that first one, a blue LTD station wagon." The sleek El Dorado Carolyn drives now often helps her make contacts; the license plates read FREE CAR.

It wasn't "natural" for Carolyn to own nice things. "I was raised in a religion where you weren't supposed to have any money," she explains, "and my family really believed. We never had any money." In Carolyn's upbringing, money was something no one talked about. Maybe that's why it was easier for her to sell the products than it was to sell the business opportunities. It was Carolyn's desire to help others that finally made it possible for her to break through her ingrained reluctance to talk about money. "It made me mad to see that the economy was so bad that young people couldn't own homes and old people couldn't retire and the people caught in the middle were just plain running scared. So then I became comfortable crusading about how Shaklee offered people an opportunity to have what they needed—and some luxuries as well."

After she was working full time with Shaklee, Carolyn realized other bonuses; one was her freedom to be with the children when they needed her. And she found time now to become involved in activities that were important to them. "I always said that someday I would be PTA president for my kids. I remembered when I ran for student council president in junior high. The vote was tied, so the teacher broke the tie by voting for the other girl—her mother was president of the PTA!" Now Carolyn found she had the freedom to budget her own time and do those things that were important to her.

As Carolyn's business grew, she needed more office space than was available in her small rented house. She rejected the idea of renting office space in favor of buying a larger house with an extra room for an office. She found the ideal house in Bellhurst, a housing project whose developer had run out of money. Since the houses were only partially completed, they were relatively inexpensive. Carolyn put down a $500 deposit and went to her bank to borrow an additional $4,000 to complete construction.

Not only did her bank refuse her the loan, but every bank she went to refused her. As an unmarried woman without a fixed salary, she was classified as a poor credit risk, despite the fact that now, her third year with Shaklee, she was earning about $1,500 a month.

Knowing she could not get the house and would lose her $500 deposit, Carolyn was depressed that night when she called Bob Ewing to talk business. Finally he asked, "What's wrong?"

Carolyn explained the situation to him, and Bob asked, "How much do you need?"

"Four thousand dollars."

"Do you want to come over here to get it, or shall I send it out to you?"

"I broke down and cried when he said that," she says. "Why, I never even asked my folks for a penny in my life, let alone someone else."

The new home soon became too small for Carolyn's expanding business. She began to rent large halls for her sales meetings. From that point to this day, her career and her life have zoomed along on an upward path. Her people are now serviced from a training center in a 2,500-square-foot office located in a Huntington Beach shopping center on the Pacific Coast Highway.

Life for Carolyn today is vastly different than it was fourteen years ago when she became a Shaklee Distributor. Her children are grown—and healthy. And she is now happily married.

Don Spargur and Carolyn were married for several years before he sold his successful motorcycle dealership in 1975 to join her in Shaklee. A well-built man of medium height, Don believes as much as Carolyn does in health and fitness, and looks considerably younger than his fifty years. In fact, with his dark hair and mustache, he is sometimes compared to Burt Reynolds. (Carolyn, incidentally, strongly resembles Dyan Cannon and has been asked to sign autographs.)

Don thoroughly enjoys their Shaklee business in comparison to the business he sold. "For one thing," he says in his quiet voice, "that was a seven-day-a-week job. And there were all kinds of employee problems." Don finds the customer response very different, too. "Customers are always thanking us, instead of complaining that this part didn't work or that machine broke down. After that, Shaklee is what I consider a problem-free business. It's a real pleasure to be in it."

Don's quiet ways are a contrast to Carolyn's outspoken enthusiasm. Although he has developed a real talent for public speaking, he still considers her the best person to talk to potential Distributors. When people ask him about the business, he takes their name and phone number and tells them that Carolyn will call. Carolyn never underestimates Don's contribution to their incredible success. However, Don tells his audiences, "If you guys want a sure-fire way to succeed in this business, marry a Key Coordinator."

The Spargurs live in Sunset Beach in an ocean-front dream house. They bought an existing home and have added rooms and levels around and above it. The 10,000-square-foot structure is entered through double doors with a large S logo that, Don explains, "stands for Shaklee and Spargur." Inside the doors, an atrium encloses a full-size tree. Many oil paintings by Carolyn, who is an accomplished artist, are displayed throughout the house. The marine room overlooking the waterfront has a view of Catalina, twenty-two miles away. This room centers on an often-used barbecue that Don designed and built. On the second floor, the master bedroom also fronts on the water; the adjoining bathroom holds a family-size Jacuzzi and sauna. Everywhere in the house, which is worth over $1 million, fine craftsmanship is evident in the beautiful woods used for paneling and molding.

The pride and joy of the Spargurs' house is the third floor, which is large enough for Don and Carolyn to hold meetings for 250 Shaklee people at a time. Naturally, these meetings draw the curious as well as people in their own group. Carolyn once overheard a woman in the beauty shop saying, "She's somebody important in Shaklee. You've got to see the house Dr. Shaklee built for that woman!"

Even though the monthly influx of people means quite a lot of traffic as newcomers "take the grand tour," Carolyn and Don would never think of closing their house to Shaklee people. Recently someone asked Carolyn, "How can you stand having all those people traipse through your house and over that white carpeting?"

"Those people," Carolyn replied, "are the reason I *have* this beautiful home and white carpeting."

The original part of the house is now a self-contained apartment, which the Spargurs rent to Dianna and Don Roach. Don, now in his mid-forties, has been a quadriplegic since he was eighteen, with limited ability to use his hands. A highly intelligent man, Don had previously been successful in the restaurant business. Today, however, thanks to the Spargurs, he is a member of the Shaklee family.

Since Don and Dianna became Distributors, their progress has been a delight to the Spargurs. The only problem was that Don wanted badly to attend meetings on the top level, but it was too difficult to transport his wheelchair up the winding staircase that leads from the ground floor.

Finally one day Carolyn said, "Don, it's a shame we can't get you up here. I'll tell you what. When you make Coordinator, we'll put in an elevator."

With the elevator as special incentive, Don and Dianna went full steam ahead, and quickly reached the rank of Coordinator. Although the Spargurs were shocked to learn that a custom-built elevator costs over $18,000, Carolyn is happy and proud to have kept her part of the bargain.

Carolyn points out that this concern is typical of Shaklee. When the Roaches qualified for a bonus car, Shaklee had it equipped with special controls so Don could drive it. And when the Roaches attended a New Supervisors Convention in San Francisco, they had a special itinerary and were given special treatment all the time. A trained driver was waiting to help Don off the plane, and a van with a lift was at the couple's disposal. Their room at the Hilton had wide doors and an extra large bathroom. "It has to be that way," Carolyn explains. "Our philosophy is that Shaklee is for everybody, so naturally the company makes allowances for people who need special attention."

Another member of the Spargur branch of the Shaklee family is Carolyn's mother. She too had needed special attention. In 1969, when Carolyn was just starting in Shaklee, "Mom had already had two heart attacks that did quite a bit of damage. Well, when I started using Shaklee products, of course I thought of her. There she was, needing help to get out of bed in the morning; she couldn't do anything herself. She was on a dozen medications, surrounded by doctors. I called and wrote about Shaklee, but she just wouldn't listen."

So Carolyn flew out to Oklahoma to see her mother, bringing along a suitcase full of Shaklee products, practically all the stock she owned. With her mother a captive audience in bed, Carolyn gathered a few relatives and neighbors and talked Shaklee with all the conviction she had.

While her mother remained skeptical, Carolyn's father was interested enough to think about going into Shaklee. He and Carolyn each contributed $100 for an ad in the Tulsa newspaper and a room at a local hotel. The ad ran for six days and Carolyn stood by the phone, but nobody called. Still, she and her relatives went ahead with the building of a big display for the great night.

On the night of the meeting, Carolyn's mother was so upset by all the activity that she stayed home. Most of the ten dollars' worth of coffee brought in was thrown out, because the only people who showed up for the meeting were three relatives, a waitress from the hotel dining room, and the elevator operator. "I cried all night," Carolyn says. "I'd wasted my money and my father's, and he didn't have much more than I did."

Down-hearted, Carolyn left the products with her parents and went home. All she had managed to accomplish by the trip was to convince her mother to take half a Vita-Lea and Vita-E each day and a pinch of Instant Protein.

Then, two weeks later, Carolyn's sister called from Oklahoma City. Carolyn's heart sank, for the calls usually meant their mother was not well. "Is it Mother?" she asked.

"Yes," said her sister. "There's going to be another Shaklee meeting in Tulsa, and Mother is giving it!"

Carolyn had heard stories about this happening to Shaklee people, but this was the first time it had happened to her. She immediately called her mother to congratulate her. She went on to say, "Mother, if that little bit does so much, think of what four Vita-Leas would do."

"Now, Carolyn."

Her mother's acceptance of nutritional supplements was steady. Her progress was so remarkable that people who knew her said, "Whatever you're taking, I want some of it, too."

Carolyn remembers the phone call when her mother asked her to send "some more of that powder stuff," the Instant Protein.

"But Mom," Carolyn said, "You told me nobody in Oklahoma would pay six dollars for a can of anything."

"Just send it dear, please."

Carolyn's parents' success has been heartwarming. They have received six bonus cars and have qualified for every convention since they joined; now Shaklee conventions all over the world are occasions for family reunions. Carolyn's parents just retired in a California condominium not far from the Spargurs. They enjoy a fine monthly retirement income from their Shaklee business.

"This business literally kept Mom alive," Carolyn reflects. "If my only reward had been to see Mom and Dad get so much out of the business, that would have been more than enough."

For all their success and happiness, Carolyn and Don Spargur are not through dreaming. At the beginning of each year they sit down and talk about their goals, and then commit them to paper in a manner that takes advantage of Carolyn's artistic ability. She draws pictures on a 20" × 30" poster to create what she calls a "dream workboard."

Past dream workboards have included such items as a beach house, a Bertram fishing boat, and an El Dorado convertible. To get the car, the Spargurs had to become Masters. The dream workboard gave them direction, and they achieved that goal within a year. Another item that has appeared regularly on the dream workboard is the Altus Award. This original blown-glass sculpture is named after the mythical bird that soars the highest, and it is presented annually at the ICC to those teams that gain membership in Shaklee's prestigious Presidents' Club.

After the first Presidents' Club presentation in 1979 in Vienna, the Spargurs set a goal of being in the Presidents' Club in 1980 and being number one in 1981. They received their first Altus in 1980 for being in the category of people who had the most net gain in First, Second, and Third Levels during the year. In 1981 they were number one in that category. They also came in first in another category, for having the greatest net gain of all First Level Sales Leaders. The Spargurs find that pictures, such as that of the Altus, on their dream workboard help form strong visual images in their minds and keep them working toward the goals they want to reach.

Many people comment on the obvious warmth between Don and Carolyn—more typical of honeymooners than of a couple married ten years. As Don comments, "It's awfully easy to feel we're on a honeymoon when everything we dream of becomes a reality."

While both the Spargurs derive a great deal of pleasure from their house, cars, jewelry, and other possessions, they cannot forget that their excellent health is one of the most important things Shaklee has brought them. Carolyn remarks, "From the very beginning when you start with Shaklee you begin to be health-conscious. You notice gradual changes in yourself until one day you're entirely a new person. I've seen it happen with everybody who practices what Shaklee stands for. *Shaklee is the greatest self-improvement program in the world!*"

7

The Rewards of Persistence
(*The Simecka Story*)

AFTER LIVING in California for two years, Don and Pat Simecka almost left the state without ever having heard of Shaklee. They were relocating to Denver, Pat's hometown. Tired of his job with the Foreign Study Program of Transamerica, Don had accepted a position selling recreational real estate in the Colorado mountains. On June 18, 1971, he made his last calls on the Southern California educators he had worked with.

Myron Kirsch, associate superintendent of the Garden Grove school district, was one of many people Don was sorry to say goodbye to. An experienced administrator with a doctorate, Myron was a person Don respected and had enjoyed working with.

As Don entered Myron's office at the end of the day, his curiosity was aroused. Myron was drawing a neat X through June 18 on his calendar, and the expression on his face indicated that drawing that big X was very satisfying.

Myron put the calendar aside and smiled. "Only twelve more days."

"Until what?" Don asked, seating himself in the chair beside the desk.

"On June thirtieth I take early retirement."

"No kidding! What are you going to do?"

"I'm going to join Gerri, my wife, in her business."

Gerri, Don knew, did something lucrative and always drove a new car. But he had never been curious enough to find out just what it was.

"Don," Myron said thoughtfully, "it's amazing. She's only been building that business for four and a half years, and she could retire today with a higher income than I will retire on. And I've been in the school system for twenty-three years."

"What is her business?"

"Shaklee. You know, Don, this is something you really must look into. Why don't you come over to our house Sunday?"

"Actually, we're moving Monday morning." But Myron's conviction about the business piqued Don's curiosity. He agreed to visit the Kirsches for just one hour on Sunday. It would be a break from the packing the Simeckas would be doing that day.

While Don's enthusiasm for the Sunday visit was mild, his wife Pat's was nonexistent. There were a thousand things to do before the long drive to Denver began the next morning at dawn. "I never heard of this Shaklee," Pat protested.

Don explained what little he knew. His wife was still not enthusiastic. She had no interest in vitamins and even less interest in selling anything. Today her green eyes dance with laughter when she recalls her reaction. "To put it mildly, I *didn't* have the Shaklee mentality."

"Pat, at least we ought to take a look," Don argued. "Myron is giving up a very good position for this. I have a lot of respect for that man. He must know what he's doing. We owe it to ourselves to hear him out."

"One hour?" Pat asked.

"Just one hour."

Reluctantly, Pat agreed. The young couple arrived at the Kirsches' at four for what turned out to be a "Shaklee hour." Their meeting didn't break up until after seven.

Pat, distracted by moving plans, tried to listen politely, all the while wondering, Why are we doing this? Gerri and Pat chatted inside the house while the men talked on the porch. Myron told Don very little about the marketing plan; what he remembers best is seeing a monthly bonus check for $5,000.

Although that check was intriguing, the Simeckas, about to embark on a new life, were cautious about getting involved. They had nothing to lose, so they became Distributors but bought only a quart of Basic-H and a tube of toothpaste to take with them, for a total cost of $2.71. Myron urged them to try food supplements, but seeing their reluctance, Gerri reminded him that the Simeckas had no room in their little Mustang. She gave Pat some Shaklee literature, which Pat tucked in her handbag.

The Simeckas weren't prepared to invest in a business. Pat had given up her job as a schoolteacher and did not know what she'd find in Denver. They would have to live on what they had saved until Don's real estate commissions produced an adequate income. The move was something they both wanted, and they hoped that real estate held the kind of opportunity Don was looking for; but it was a plunge into unknown waters.

As Pat said during the trip, if nothing else came of the Shaklee distributorship, at least they could purchase the products they might want at wholesale. She had liked the Kirsches, and their conviction about the products had impressed her.

Once they were settled in Denver, Pat made further inquiries about teaching jobs and confirmed her fears; nothing was available. She was able to get referrals of students who needed special tutoring in reading. That brought in some extra money but didn't fill her time.

She laughs. "Today I can't imagine 'killing time.' But that's why I started reading the Shaklee literature, just to kill some time." The material appealed to her, and what she read about the marketing plan brought back the memory of that $5,000 bonus check. Don was doing well for a new real estate agent, but they were not realizing their previous income. Pat wanted to do something more to take the burden off him.

"To this day I don't know what made me do it," she says with an engaging smile, "but I sent Gerri an order for $300 worth of products."

Without any idea of how to sell, Pat made up a list of everyone she had ever known in Denver. "When I think of it today," she says, "I'm surprised I had the courage. But it turned out to be the right thing to do. Now I tell new people, 'Don't wait until you've attended every training class and read all the sales material. You don't have time to do all that. Time is of the essence. Just jump right in and see people.'"

Making those first calls wasn't easy, but the sight of $300 worth of products stacked in the living room spurred Pat on. Whether or not she continued with Shaklee, she at least had to recoup her investment. As she says, "I began making those calls out of sheer fright! Every time I needed some motivation I'd just take a look at all those products."

At first Pat felt awkward calling people she hadn't seen since she left Denver seven years ago. Still, she forced herself to make the calls. Instinctively she developed a low-key approach, chatting with each person a few minutes and then saying, "I've started a business. I'd like to tell you about it." She never tried to tell anyone about Shaklee on the telephone, but always asked when she could visit and explain the business in person.

Although Pat knew she would face rejections, it wasn't easy. When she recalls her reaction in those days, her cheeks redden a little. "It was especially tough when I called someone who had been an adult when I was a child. I'd always think, Boy, if anybody will be happy to see me it's this person, because she knew me when I was a little kid. When someone like that rejected me, it really hurt. Today I realize that they weren't rejecting *me*, or even the products. They didn't understand what the business was about. But then I was so green that I took the rejections very personally."

Sometimes Pat was so hurt and discouraged she broke into tears. Don remembers one crucial night when he came home to discover his wife sitting on the couch crying. "I can't do this," she sobbed. "I just don't think this business is for me. I can't do it."

Don, a calm, thoughtful man, could see how shaken Pat was by the rejections she was receiving. "Pat," he said, "if this is upsetting you so much, maybe you should just let it go."

"Oh, no!" she cried. "I can't let it go. I must make it work!" For all her disappointments, Pat realized at that moment that she was building something that was hers.

While Pat's career was off to a somewhat shaky start, Don was doing well selling recreational mountain properties. The problem was that it was a seven-day-a-week job. Since the properties were in the southern portion of the state, about two and a half hours from Denver, most people wanted to see them on weekends. As the months went on, Don felt more and more fatigued and overburdened. He was supportive of Pat's work, but had neither the time nor energy to help.

Pat communicated regularly with Gerri Kirsch. She recorded her questions on cassette tapes and mailed them to Gerri in California; Gerri called long-distance with answers and pep talks. Pat's inquiries were often long and elaborate. Why did people need food supplements at all? Why Shaklee instead of some other brand? How did the skin care products work?

"Gerri was terrific," Pat says, dimpling as she smiles. "She never failed to answer my questions right away."

But for all Gerri's help and Don's support, Pat was confused and discouraged. Five months after she began the business she sent her California Supervisor a long tape. She still had so many questions she was beginning to think she would never learn the business.

A few days later Gerri called. "I got your tape yesterday," she said, "and you sounded so desperate I couldn't sleep last night. I'm coming to Denver to help you."

Pat considered Gerri's visit an extraordinary act of kindness. Certainly Pat's low purchase volume did not warrant the substantial expense of flying from California to Denver. Moreover, this was Gerri's first business trip without Myron. Because she was uneasy traveling alone, she brought her secretary—another round-trip air fare. All this was for a woman Gerri had met only once (in fact, Pat was afraid she might not recognize Gerri at the airport).

Gerri and her secretary stayed at the Simecka house for nearly a week, and, as Pat recalls, "We never slept! We talked for eighteen hours a day." Gerri reviewed every facet of the business while Pat tape-recorded everything she said. Gerri went over the material until she was certain that Pat understood and felt secure. She covered the products, the sales program, and Shaklee's philosophy.

"I can't believe her patience," Pat says.

The two women developed a strong friendship during the visit. Gerri felt close enough to express her concern about Don. "That man is killing himself," she said. "He's just working too hard—from early morning until late at night." In fact, Don was beginning to wonder about the wisdom of choosing this new career. True, he was doing well, but it hardly seemed worth the price.

For Pat, Gerri's visit came at the perfect time. Such a visit would have been less valuable during Pat's first weeks as a Distributor, when she had too little experience to even know what questions to ask. "But if she had waited long to come," Pat says thoughtfully, "I might have become too discouraged and quit." As it was, Pat might not have been in love with Shaklee when Gerri came, but she certainly was by the time the women said goodbye.

After Gerri left, Pat approached her business with new gusto. Until now, Pat had concentrated on selling to retail customers and sponsored very few Distributors. Now she began to turn these retail customers into Distributors. When she delivered the second order to a satisfied customer, she

might say, "You know, you're just the kind of person I'm looking for in this business. You'd be absolutely great doing what
I'm doing." If a good retail customer complained, "I'd like
to buy this month, but I really can't afford to," Pat would
reply, "You really should become a Distributor. Then you can
buy all these products for your family at wholesale prices."
If the customer replied that he just wasn't interested, she
would say softly, "Okay. But why don't you just think about
it? I'll get in touch with you again." Her neat records insured
that she would remember to follow up and call the potential
Distributor again and again. Pat's personal sales philosophy
was now developing too, and it already included an emphasis
on service and on persistence. This persistence, coupled with
her gentle manner and enthusiastic presentation, began to
show results, and Pat signed up more and more Distributors.

By May of 1973 Pat was in full gear, and some of her
Distributors were beginning to build their businesses too. One
evening she called Gerri to place an $800 emergency order.
The next day Gerri phoned. Pat was away and Don took the
call. "Don, last night after I got Pat's order I added up her
PV for the past three months. She has qualified for Supervisor."

When Pat came home that evening, Don told her to sit
down. He chuckles to remember that on that day, for the
first time, he took a proprietary interest in the business. "Pat,
we made Supervisor."

Pat's response was immediate: "Oh no, Don. I don't want
it, I don't want it."

Don was surprised. "What you'd better do," he said, "is
call Gerri and talk to her about it."

Reluctantly, Pat placed the call.

"But why not?" Gerri asked, somewhat stunned.

"Gerri, I'm not sure I can hold on to this. I'm not sure I
can do it."

"You're already doing it. You do everything a Supervisor
does already. Don't you want to get paid for it?"

"I just don't know if I can hold on to it," Pat repeated miserably. "And what happens if I revert?"

"Pat, *I'm* not going to tell anybody! And I promise to stay in close touch with you," she said.

Don grins at the recollection. "I think Pat believed that if she failed, the news would be on the front page of the *Denver Post* and the *Rocky Mountain News:* 'Pat Simecka from Littleton has reverted from a Shaklee Supervisor to a Distributor!' Actually, at the time there were very few people in Denver who would have known what that meant!"

But whatever Pat's fears, Gerri had allayed them. Pat gathered her courage and, to Don's delight, told Gerri, "All right, I'll do it!"

Now that she was a Supervisor, Pat was more determined than ever to succeed. Her 1099 tax form for 1973 shows that she earned $6,600. The following year, her first full year as Supervisor, her income leapt to $18,000—almost triple what she had earned as a schoolteacher.

At the same time, Don was becoming more and more disenchanted with his position in real estate. The long hours burned him out, and he didn't enjoy the work. "I had figured out a way to make money," he says with a sigh, "but I hadn't figured out a way to really live." His discontent was fueled by a Shaklee mini-convention at Colorado Springs which he attended with Pat in February 1974. At the all-day workshop, a top Sales Leader gave a crystal-clear presentation of the Sales Plan. "Until that point," Don says, "neither Pat nor I really understood the fine points. But after he finished explaining, we looked at each other and whispered, 'My gosh, what are we sitting on?' "

Several months later, after nearly three grueling years in real estate, Don resigned from his job. Hindsight suggests that the time was right for him to join his wife in building their Shaklee business, but that was not yet obvious to the Simeckas. As a bright young salesman with a good track record, Don received numerous phone calls from interested companies, and he went to one interview after another.

But in each position, some vital spark was lacking. Unable to work up enthusiasm for the job, Don would say, "Thank you very much, but don't call me. I'll call you."

"I just couldn't get excited about those jobs," he says today, "when I knew there was more going on in our basement than in any of those places!"

Finally an offer from Don's previous company brought the Simeckas to a crossroads. The Foreign Study League, now under new ownership, offered him the San Francisco territory and a base salary of $25,000. It was a dream job, but what about Pat's career?

Don called Myron Kirsch for his advice. "What do you think would happen to Pat's business if I took that job in San Francisco and we relocated?"

Myron deliberated and then answered, "I think it will hurt her business. Her organization will suffer."

Then Myron, a careful, logical thinker, offered a suggestion. "Don, why don't you do the old Ben Franklin balance sheet? Write down all the pros and cons for taking that job, and then write down all the pros and cons for staying with Shaklee. And then write down the things that you really want in this life. It won't be difficult to make your decision."

So, for the first time in their lives, the Simeckas put their lifetime goals on paper. "And do you know what?" Don asks. "It became very clear that Shaklee fulfilled every possibility."

Don refused the job offer and joined Pat in Shaklee. It was a bold decision, since his earnings had accounted for over half the family income. "There were a lot of ifs," Don says quietly. "*If* the business worked. *If* the people kept coming. *If* the Distributors kept sponsoring. But we decided to bag up that little word 'if' and throw it away. We began to say 'when.' We decided it was going to work for us. In other words, we made a commitment."

The Simeckas' commitment to the business meant sacrifice. For a year they would not be able to buy anything except absolute necessities. But they were still young and willing to do without, because, as Pat says, "we knew that eventually this business would be very profitable. We both knew it would work, because we had seen it work for other people. And we knew that if *we* worked very hard, it would work for us, too."

In his speeches today, Don advises men who join their wives' businesses to have more specific game plans than he did. "Not knowing what to do," he admits with a wry smile, "I decided to be Pat's bookkeeper and well-paid stock boy. For the first eight months I stayed in the office. I undoubtedly would have been better off on the golf course, because then I would have at least made some contacts!" At least Don's work in the office freed Pat for more of the outside work she loved. Moreover, during those first months Don learned the workings of the business thoroughly; and the more he learned, the more enthusiastic he became.

Eventually the time came for Don to pull his own weight. Alone, he traveled through Kansas calling on old friends to tell them about Shaklee. In the course of the trip, he sponsored a number of people, including two old buddies from his college basketball days. Both men and their wives built their businesses until one couple reached Supervisor and the other Assistant Supervisor. In addition, one of the couples sponsored another couple who went on to become Supervisors.

At the time, the results of Don's trip to Kansas were not yet in. So it was not until January 1975 that he felt he was beginning to make a major contribution to the business, when he and Pat sat down and wrote out their strategy for the future. They fixed a figure as the minimum volume that they had to make to survive, and they made a joint commitment to concentrate on building the four sales teams in their organization. The Simeckas established goals for their Distributors and constantly motivated them to excel. Their efforts paid off. In September, Don and Pat became Coordinators. Only two years later they became Key Coordinators.

The fact that Don joined Pat gave the business new life. "People took the business more seriously," she explains, "when they saw it was good enough for Don to do." Don and Pat worked well together. Don had been supportive of Pat's career long before he joined her. "It takes a very secure man not to be threatened by his wife's prosperity," Pat comments. But Don had never felt threatened. As he explains: "Regardless of who earns the money, it all ends up in the same funnel."

Taking Don's hand, Pat adds, "I treasure the time we spend together. It's just great to know we wake up in the morning with a common goal. We're working in harmony and building something we'll share for the rest of our lives. That's very dear to me.

"Sometimes I find myself taking for granted the time we spend together, until I look at some of my friends whose husbands are always out of town on business trips. Even couples whose work doesn't require any travel don't see that much of each other. They're separated from eight in the morning until six or seven at night. Working together has made our marriage all the better. I do think that if a marriage is weak to begin with, working together may drive people further apart. But if a marriage is basically strong, it will get stronger."

Don and Pat sometimes travel separately, but they do most of their traveling together. They feel Shaklee is so much fun that a business-centered trip is not exhausting but thoroughly enjoyable. In 1978 they took a month-long "multipurpose" trip around the country, visiting friends and relatives they hadn't seen for a while. At the same time, as Don says with a grin, "We talked Shaklee wherever we went." Of the Distributors the Simeckas sponsored during that trip, seven have gone on to become Supervisors. While the Simeckas have not computed the bonuses ultimately generated by their trip, the figure would certainly run into the tens of thousands of dollars.

Since they became a Shaklee team, the Simeckas have also

traveled all over the world to company conventions. They especially remember the convention in Acapulco in 1976, their first Coordinators Convention. One evening as they were having dinner with Gerri and Myron Kirsch, Myron rose and called for a toast. "When Pat and Don make Masters," he said, "Gerri and I want them to get their passports ready." Intrigued, Don and Pat asked what he meant, but Myron refused to say more.

In May 1980 the Simeckas became Master Coordinators. In the four years since Myron's toast nothing more had been said between the two couples about it. It would have been natural, Pat and Don agreed, if the Kirsches had forgotten the toast altogether.

But once the news was released, the first people to call with congratulations were Gerri and Myron.

"Get out your passports," Myron said. "Gerri and I are sending the two of you to Hong Kong!"

As the Shaklee saying goes, "The next best thing to being a Master is having one." The Kirsches had worked hard for the Simeckas, investing time and money in long-distance phone calls, taped correspondence, and Gerri's first trip to Denver to help Pat. As a result, both couples have enjoyed prosperity. Today the Kirsches are Key Coordinators; in 1980 they received approximately $40,000 worth of bonuses generated by the Simecka organization.

Pat and Don have everything they ever dreamed about. They receive more in bonuses in one month than Pat used to earn in one year as a teacher. More than that, they enjoy knowing that at any time they could retire with built-in financial security. "In every other field," Don says, "a person works hard for forty years so he or she can take it easy for five years after retirement. But Shaklee gave us the opportunity to work hard for five years so we could take it easy for the next forty!"

The Simeckas aren't taking it easy yet—neither is yet forty years old—and they are enjoying themselves too much to quit.

But, as Pat says, "it's wonderful to be in a position where there's no financial pressure."

Experience has changed Pat and Don somewhat. As platform speakers, they know how to tell their story in a way that is witty, interesting, and yet heartfelt. They run their business with an emphasis on the details of service and follow-up that is highly professional. But their sincerity and enthusiasm are no less than in the beginning. Although they don't have to, they continue to seek out and sponsor new people.

"Why do you bother?" people often ask. "After all, *you're Masters.*"

Don replies, "The pace of the leader sets the speed of the pack," and Pat nods vigorously. She herself still spends hours at a time making phone calls, perhaps to inactive Distributors within the Simecka organization. "I had a very hard time the other day," she says. "I'm not trying to ruin the image of a Master Coordinator, but I don't think you ever get to where you don't feel call reluctance from time to time. The only way to get over it is to *do* it."

Obviously, success has not spoiled Pat and Don. They have retained their modesty and their willingness to work. Their enthusiasm is at an all-time high. They are not willing to settle for the status quo but are working toward new goals. "We haven't even begun to tap the potential in Shaklee," Don says.

Pat agrees. "We're not going to slow down." Then her dimples appear as she smiles. "The truth is, we're having too much fun to say, 'Hey, we've arrived.' "

8

"Behind Every Successful Woman . . ." (*The Boltinghouse Story*)

FOR AS LONG as she can remember, JoAnn Boltinghouse had an overwhelming desire to be successful. "I was adopted," the petite blonde says, "and I felt so grateful to my parents I always wanted to do something extraordinary to live up to what I thought they expected of me. But I was never the best at anything. In school I was the homecoming queen's *attendant*. I was *secretary* of my school class, never president. I married well—but then I was sharing my husband's success. I was *Mrs.* Dr. Earl Boltinghouse.

"I kept working hard, trying for my own piece of glory. I was a first-grade teacher in my hometown of Harlan, Iowa. I was the Sunday School superintendent at my church. I was the chairman of the Community Chest drive. I was—I am—the mother of three wonderful children—Jeff, Kerry, and Ginger. And still I felt the need for something more. I felt I had great reserves of potential inside me that were going untapped."

Eventually JoAnn would tap these reserves and become one of Shaklee's top Sales Leaders. But this success came only after considerable hesitation. At first, in fact, she was reluctant to talk about Shaklee products with her friends.

JoAnn had no desire to sell anything to her friends, and with good reason. Several years before she had purchased a large suitcase of lingerie from a party plan company for nearly a thousand dollars. "I discovered I wasn't that much of a salesperson," she says with a laugh. "I ended up stuck with a whole case of bras that weren't even my size.

"Of course, I should have known I was no saleswoman. Every time the church had a chicken dinner, I was asked to sell ten tickets. I'd buy all ten because I didn't have the nerve to ask anyone to buy them!"

The Boltinghouses were introduced to Shaklee through a friend and dental patient of Earl's, Mavis Thief, who brought some products to his office. Earl was unenthusiastic, but he bought some Basic-H and some skin care products, reasoning, "What the heck, JoAnn can always use the stuff at home."

JoAnn, who had always had a problem complexion, got phenomenal results from the skin care program, especially when she used it in conjunction with Shaklee nutritional products. A friend commented to her, "Gee, JoAnn, your face looks better. What are you doing?"

"Oh, it's some of that stuff Mavis sells," JoAnn replied, and hurried on to another topic.

Each time JoAnn ordered new supplies, Mavis tried talking her into becoming a Distributor. Mavis felt that JoAnn's warmth and vitality would make her excellent Shaklee material. Every time JoAnn got her supplies she found a Distributor's application and a little note reading, "You ought to let me sponsor you."

"I tore up more Distributor's applications than anyone in the history of the company," JoAnn says with a laugh. "And if *I* hadn't torn them up, *he* would have." She points at Earl. The memory of the lingerie investment stayed with Earl. He kept reminding JoAnn, "You know what happened the last time you tried to sell something. You're *not* going to sign that paper!"

For a long time Earl wouldn't even try Shaklee Nutritional

Products. As a dentist, he got loads of free samples from drug salesmen. He tried many of these pills because he didn't feel in top condition. His insurance physical showed he was healthy, but he usually needed a midday nap just to keep going. However, he found that the products the salesmen sent him tasted bad, upset his stomach, or just didn't help. "Mavis kept chipping away at us," he comments. "Pretty soon I began to think that if the other products we were using had such high quality, I should at least try Shaklee Nutritional Products."

Convincing Earl was not an easy matter, although the products worked for him. He was coming home at the end of the day with energy to spare, and he stopped taking naps. "Then," he says with a slightly sheepish smile, "I figured, 'Wait a minute. This is all in my head. I've got it all together now, and that's why I'm feeling better. I don't need these products anymore.' " But once he dispensed with the program, Earl found himself napping again. "That did it," he says. "I started taking Shaklee and feeling great, and I haven't quit since."

Once Earl was a believer, he agreed that buying wholesale was a good idea. On January 11, 1971, JoAnn was sponsored into Shaklee. "Thank heaven for Mavis's persistence!" she says with a contented smile.

JoAnn was still uncomfortable with the idea of selling, but she found that sometimes using the products led to selling them. She took Basic-H to school to clean the children's chairs, and found herself surrounded by other teachers who marveled at how well it worked. Almost reluctantly, JoAnn took orders for the product.

She was much happier sponsoring new Distributors at evening gatherings. JoAnn asked friends to host little gatherings of six or eight women where she could demonstrate Shaklee products. "I was teaching full-time," she explains, "and running a household with three children. So I wanted to accomplish as much as I could in my Shaklee time. Group presentations seemed to utilize my time best."

Characteristically, JoAnn was more interested in sharing her enthusiasm than in making money. She often offered the hostess a small gift, such as a coffee maker, and sometimes even gave the hostess all the profits on the orders! "I had a hangup about selling," she repeats.

In May 1971 JoAnn and a friend drove to Council Bluffs, Iowa, to her first Shaklee meeting. At the meeting JoAnn was handed her first bonus check. She was so excited that she talked Shaklee all the way back. When she got home after midnight, she immediately woke Earl to tell him all about it. He peered at the check and said, "Four dollars and fifty-eight cents! Do you mean you drove over a hundred miles for *that?*"

During the summer vacation, JoAnn's Shaklee business began to pick up, even though her schedule was hectic. She was driving a hundred miles a day to take college courses toward a degree in psychology. As her classes began at 7:00 A.M., she had to leave the house before six. When she got home, she had to fit in her Shaklee business between her studies, the housework, and time spent with the children. JoAnn even had time to paint her living room. "But I made Assistant Supervisor that summer," she says proudly. "So when people tell me they're too busy for Shaklee, I know they could still do it if they wanted to. As the saying goes, 'Where there's a will, there's a way.' "

In the fall JoAnn went back to teaching full-time; but she also promised herself to devote two evenings a week to giving Shaklee presentations. At about this time she learned that Dr. Shaklee would be featured at a meeting in Minneapolis, and that anyone in her group with enough Purchase Volume would win a paid motel room for the weekend. JoAnn determined to win the free lodging, and she did.

At the meeting, Earl and JoAnn saw "some bonus checks a lot bigger than $4.58," he recalls. "And for the first time I saw the business opportunity in Shaklee."

"Then and there, somewhere in the back of my mind, I

formed a goal," JoAnn says. "I wanted to be the first Master in Dr. Shaklee's home state of Iowa, and have him come to Harlan to pin me. I finally had a clear goal to aim for, and the way to achieve it was spelled out step by step—by achieving the positions of Supervisor, Coordinator, Key Coordinator, and then Master. So I had the challenge and, most important, *I had the direction.*"

With her enthusiasm reinforced by the Minneapolis meeting, and with Earl's full support, JoAnn made Supervisor a month later in November 1971. Although she was still teaching full-time, her PV was $6,000, and she received a bonus check for over $1,400. She credits her success to consistency. "It's the number one quality you need to build a Shaklee business," she states firmly. "I gave two presentations every single week, no matter what."

The next summer was very special to JoAnn. "That new Supervisors Convention in San Francisco had to be one of the biggest thrills we've ever had in Shaklee," she says. "Instead of taking the plane tickets, Earl and I took the money and drove out with our three children. It was our first long, luxurious vacation. We got to see a lot of the country, Disneyland and San Francisco. And we met so many wonderful people!"

JoAnn was so excited by the convention that she wanted everyone in her organization to become a Supervisor. "But none of my Distributors *wanted* to become Supervisors," she says. "They saw me running around doing all these things, and they didn't want to work that hard."

The problem was that JoAnn had told her people about Shaklee products, but had never fully explained the business opportunities to them. In consequence, she had many people who were "users—but not doers."

The business was lopsided, Earl explains, holding up his hands as if they formed a balance. "If you push the products too much, your people won't be interested in the business opportunity. Likewise, if you share only the opportunity, they won't have the conviction for the products. You've got to have balance."

JoAnn decided to concentrate on those people in her organization who believed the most strongly in the products, those who used them daily. These people had bought from JoAnn and Earl originally because the couple had credibility. "But they bought again," JoAnn explains, "because they thought the products performed well. This made them believers. So then it was relatively easy to explain the business opportunity to them and convince them to share with others."

The Boltinghouse organization is not, of course, confined to the town of Harlan, but spreads across the United States. It has grown, Earl says, by means of "a credibility chain. That credibility is really essential to growth. You can only sell to people who find you credible. That's the difference between selling to a friend or to a stranger. When we call on a friend, we can sit down and he or she will be open."

Today there are eleven Sales Leaders in Harlan alone. Five of them drive bonus cars. Several more Leaders live in the smaller outlying towns and villages. The success of the Boltinghouse organization, based in a town of 5,000 people with a trade area of 17,000 is amazing. They have fifty-one Supervisors and an estimated 8,000 to 10,000 Distributors from all walks of life, including executives, physicians, dentists, teachers, ministers, and farmers.

Two large groups in the Boltinghouse organization are good examples of the growth potential of the credibility chain. One group, in Wisconsin, began at a dental seminar JoAnn attended with Earl. Dr. Neil Brahe delivered such a powerful speech that JoAnn went up to thank him. She ended up sponsoring him. Through her association with Dr. Brahe, she has made so many contacts in Wisconsin that she takes three week-long trips there each year.

The Boltinghouse group in Indiana began when JoAnn sponsored her cousins, Donna and Jerry Cox, who live in Indianapolis. "It gives me a good opportunity to mix business with pleasure when I visit them," JoAnn explains.

Although JoAnn did meet Neil Brahe at a dental seminar, she rarely uses these occasions for prospecting. After the Minneapolis convention JoAnn and Earl made a list of everyone they could think of who might be Shaklee material (a selling technique they learned at that convention). That list today is "so long we haven't gotten to the bottom of it." As both JoAnn and Earl continue to add names to the list, it seems likely that they never will get to its end.

JoAnn still attends dental seminars with Earl, although as he comments, "they're awfully dull in comparison with Shaklee meetings!" Earl enjoys his work as a dentist, however, and continues to schedule a full week. One advantage of his profession is that he can arrange his schedule to travel with JoAnn and speak at some of her meetings.

But perhaps the most important advantage of Shaklee to the Boltinghouses is the income security. "In dentistry," Earl explains, "your income depends on your ability to go to work each day."

"That's right," JoAnn interjects. "If he doesn't have his hands in someone's mouth, he isn't making any money."

Grimacing, Earl admits that it's true. "When we go on vacation, nothing's happening with my dental practice. But with Shaklee we have activity going on all over the country generating income for us."

Since Harlan is a farm community, many people in the Boltinghouse organization are farmers. Farmers make good users of Shaklee products. "They understand the importance of nutrition because they know how much it affects their livestock," Earl explains. "They also make fine Distributors. Shaklee provides them with a form of income security, which they like very much, believe you me. And the Shaklee retirement plan is very appealing to them. But what makes them such good Distributors is that the husbands and wives are used to working together as teams. They're used to planning and working toward goals. They're hardworking, and they're health-conscious."

JoAnn adds, "Farmers are usually very busy people, so we don't expect them to make a full-time commitment when they're content with their present careers. But we do ask them to make a part-time commitment. I don't think that's unreasonable."

Earl is not the only Boltinghouse who is proud of JoAnn's achievements. He enjoys telling about the time their son Jeff came home from college and said, "The other kids always know exactly what their moms will be doing when they go home, but with mine, I *never* know. She may be in Hawaii, or she may be jumping out of an airplane!"

JoAnn's eyes light up when the subject of flying is mentioned. She had long wanted to fly a plane, but she did not begin lessons until her experience in Shaklee had given her the necessary sense of confidence. "And," she says proudly, "I paid for all my flight instructions with my Shaklee income." She and son Kerry were joint owners of a plane, but they sold it when he went away to college. However, now that Kerry has his commercial, instrument, and instructor's licenses, they are thinking of buying another.

A new airplane will make JoAnn's traveling considerably easier. Presently she drives about 45,000 miles a year, averaging ten to twelve meetings each week. Her record for conducting meetings is thirteen in a three-day period. "That probably sounds like a lot of work," she admits, "but not to me. I guess I'm a workaholic. It hardly seems like work to me, because I love it."

What is a typical Shaklee week for JoAnn Boltinghouse? She pulls out her date book and points at the notations. "Tonight I'll drive two and a half hours to Columbus, Nebraska, and stay overnight there for a nutrition brunch tomorrow morning. I'll come home Wednesday and on Thursday drive two hours to Sioux City—I have three meetings there. Then

I have to pick up our daughter Ginger, who's attending journalism camp at Ames, Iowa. Friday night our son's coming home from college, so I want to fix a big family dinner. Then Saturday at seven we catch a plane to Hawaii." Closing the date book with a satisfied smile, she adds, "But really, that's not so tough. I've had a lot of harder weeks."

JoAnn's calendar is also dotted with activities of her children that she plans to attend. Since Kerry is on the football team at college, football weekends are also reserved so the family can watch him play. "Having this freedom to work around my family is one of the main attractions of Shaklee to me," she says. "It was even more important when the children were small and I wanted to be home when they got home from school."

The "Shaklee lifestyle" has drawn the family together in many ways. In 1978 the Boltinghouses built a bi-level office building in Harlan; the top level houses Earl's dental practice and the bottom level is headquarters for JoAnn's Shaklee business. The building is an investment that also enables Earl to have lunch with JoAnn and to spend time in the Shaklee business between his appointments.

Until the building was constructed, the business was based in the Boltinghouse home, located five miles outside of Harlan. The house, situated on fifty acres of rolling farmland, was not designed to accommodate all the activity that goes on in a thriving Shaklee business, so JoAnn and Earl were glad to "separate our business from our private lives by putting up the building."

For JoAnn, building her Shaklee business has been a matter of stages. In 1972, when she realized that she was making more money part-time in Shaklee than she made teaching full-time, she decided to work full-time with Shaklee. But the decision to work at building a large company did not occur until five years later. "In March 1977," she explains, "we had four First Level Supervisors. That's when we made a five-year commitment to go for Master." By December 1980 the bonus recap showed thirty-four First Level Supervisors in the Boltinghouse organization—the result of two and a half years of hard work. JoAnn had realized the goal she set when she first heard Dr. Shaklee speak; in March 1978 the Boltinghouses became the first Key Coordinators in Iowa, and in May 1979 the first Masters.

Obviously this kind of growth required a great deal of hard work. "Oh, yes," JoAnn admits cheerfully, "but it was sure more fun than facing thirty first-graders every morning. I did love teaching, but it could be frustrating at times!"

Both Earl and JoAnn believe that working on Shaklee has brought the family closer together. Their daughter Ginger often works in the office along with their daughter-in-law Paula and sons Jeff and Kerry. Recently at the dinner table one of the boys summed up this particular Shaklee family by saying, "What did we ever talk about *before* we got into Shaklee?"

Every so often somebody approaches Earl at a Shaklee meeting and asks, "When did you go full-time with Shaklee?"

"I haven't," Earl replies.

"Then how did you build the business? You must really be busy!"

Far from wanting the credit for building the business, Earl sometimes feels annoyed at this assumption. "This is a business that anyone—man or woman—can build. JoAnn has done about 96 percent of it on her own, so I'll take credit for the other 4 percent."

"He says he's only done 4 percent of it," JoAnn says, "but he deserves a lot more credit than that. Earl is a wonderful sounding board. There's been many a night when I came home from a meeting or training session and we'd spend a couple of hours talking things over. If it's winter, we'll build a fire in our family room and sit around that just dreaming and planning. That's been very important to us both."

The problems that sometimes beset a couple when the woman becomes very successful have never materialized in

JoAnn and Earl's relationship. Although JoAnn is often away from home overnight, Earl never complains. "He's 100 percent supportive of everything I do," she confirms, "and believe me, that's essential to make this business a success.

"There are some men who simply can't handle their wives' success," she continues thoughtfully. "But Earl's very dedicated to his own work, and I think that makes a difference. He knows that Shaklee gives me an opportunity to be creative and to benefit people. I've grown so much. We all have."

9

A Japanese Love Affair
(*The Ara Story*)

"WE WERE WEAK, SICKLY PEOPLE," Mrs. Ara says. "My husband and I were overweight and had a number of physical complaints. My husband had hypertension, and I suffered so from low blood pressure and anemia that I could hardly get around in the morning. My elderly mother was sickly, too. Between the three of us it seemed we talked of nothing but our poor health."

Mr. Toshio Ara, sixty-one, and Mrs. Ara, fifty-six, now, however, radiate energy. Silver-haired and dressed in conservative Western clothes, both look fit and healthy. And, while they are well-mannered, soft-spoken people, their warmth and enthusiasm fill the air.

In 1976, while Mr. Ara was confined to the hospital, a friend came by with a gift of Shaklee Nutritional Products. "That's how Shaklee came into our lives," Mr. Ara explains with a little smile. "It was a gift. How could I refuse it?" The friend, who belonged to the Aras' church, had talked about Shaklee in the past, but the Aras had been skeptical. Nevertheless, all three began taking the products.

Beyond a doubt, they were feeling healthier as the months passed. Mr. Ara felt so much better he was able to discontinue some medications he had been taking. "With Shaklee," he says, "my body was being strengthened in a natural way."

Mrs. Ara and her mother experienced the same renewal of their former good health and energy by taking care of themselves and supplementing their diets with Shaklee Nutritional Products. "I was overwhelmed with joy," Mrs. Ara says. "After six months I realized how well we all felt, and I remembered how we'd been *then*. I wanted to share this joy with my friends. That's when I decided to become a Distributor."

When the Aras were sponsored in November 1976, they gave no thought to the business opportunity in Shaklee. Mrs. Ara was a former high school teacher, but there had never been any financial need for her to work. Mr. Ara, an engineer with a degree from Tokyo University, had served for nearly twenty years as Director of the Building Maintenance Department for the Japanese Ministry of Construction. Following his retirement, he took an executive position with Nippon Kokan (NKK), one of Japan's largest steel companies, a position he still holds.

An influential man who is highly respected, Mr. Ara was naturally concerned about his business reputation when he considered sharing Shaklee. He explains that there have been cases of "commercial malpractice in Japan concerning other direct sales companies." Shaklee's growing reputation in Japan, however, was very good. Moreover, Mr. Ara was comforted by the fact that when he sponsored his business colleagues they too could buy products at wholesale prices.

Mrs. Ara also appreciated the fact that her friends could become Distributors and buy Shaklee products at wholesale prices. This, she felt, enabled her to share freely her own happiness with the products. It is a testimony to Mrs. Ara's giving spirit that her greatest thrill in Shaklee has been seeing her friends feeling better through using the products. "In perhaps three to six months they really feel great!" she says excitedly. "When they tell me how happy they are, that is the response I find most rewarding."

The Shaklee Nutritional Products Line

James Scala at the Forrest C. Shaklee Research Center

Al and Joan Hegerman

Carolyn Spargur

G. R. Shuman

Pat and Don Simecka

JoAnn and Earl Boltinghouse

Noble Photography, Inc.

Mr. and Mrs. Toshio Ara
with Allan Nagle

Ted Kurihara Photography

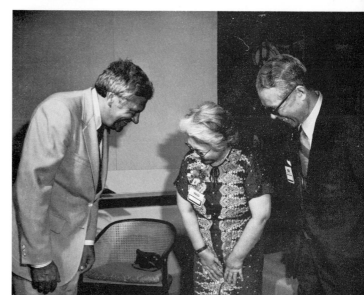

Kay and Bob Holker
and family

The Shaklee Plant at Norman, Oklahoma

Shaklee Terraces

Jack Wilder, Vice President of Sales

Claude Jarman (right), Vice President of Corporate Communications, congratulates Rock Maguire, singles champion of Shaklee Invitational Tennis Tournament

For the next eight months after they were sponsored, the Aras paid no attention to remarks they heard about the Shaklee Sales Plan. They simply continued to share their own experience with everyone they met.

Then, in the summer of 1977, Mr. and Mrs. Ara visited the Shaklee home office in Japan, where they met with Masaaki Matsushita, President of the Japanese corporation, and Ryotaro Kanzaki, Executive Director of Sales. At this meeting they learned about Dr. Shaklee and heard the company's philosophy explained in depth. Mr. Ara's respect for the company grew with this introduction to the company's history and high-quality management. Mrs. Ara felt that the Shaklee philosophy accorded with her Catholicism. "As for the philosophy of sharing," she explains, gesturing rapidly as she always does, "I didn't have to be convinced about that. I had experienced it."

Mr. Matsushita also explained the Sales Plan to the Aras at that meeting. Mrs. Ara began to see that she could share Shaklee and reap significant financial benefit at the same time. "So I set a goal to become a Sales Leader," she explains, "and kill two birds with one stone. I still felt as though I was a missionary; I just wanted to tell as many people as possible about Shaklee. But now the business opportunity was a nice extra that had been added. At this point I simply urged everybody who had experienced wonderful results to go out and share Shaklee with their friends and relatives."

Only three months after that meeting, the Aras became Supervisors, just in time for Mrs. Ara to attend the New Supervisors Convention in October in San Francisco. By this time, Mrs. Ara was so impressed with Dr. Shaklee's philosophy and products that she positively yearned to see Dr. Shaklee in person. That desire, in fact, had motivated her to become a Supervisor, and then to take the long trip to America.

"I will never forget it," she says wide-eyed. "You see, I was born right after the big earthquake that destroyed the whole Tokyo area, so I have always had a great fear of earth-

quakes. Well, we were at the banquet eating when suddenly
there was a lot of commotion and people moving around.
Immediately I jumped up and looked for the fire exit, for I
knew San Francisco also had earthquakes. Then I saw him.
Dr. Shaklee had come in, and that was what all the excitement
was about.

"Seeing him was the most memorable moment of my life.
That may sound strange, but at that moment I thought about
how the health of my mother, my husband, and myself had
changed, and about how many other people I had been able
to help with Shaklee. And there he was, Dr. Shaklee, who
had brought all these things to me. So you see," she concludes
softly, "it was very natural for me to cry with happiness."

Upon her return to Japan, Mrs. Ara was even more enthusiastic than before. She began contacting the many friends in
all parts of the country that she and Mr. Ara had made through
his work. "That enthusiasm is what is behind her success,"
says Mr. Ara. "Although I don't participate in her Shaklee
meetings, I do attend some of them with her. When I see
the audience react to her, I am fascinated. Her enthusiasm
and conviction hold them spellbound. She's always had a fine
personality, but since she joined Shaklee she has bloomed."

After her first convention Mrs. Ara began using a new
approach when she made her phone calls. She smiles broadly
as she tells about it. Her opening statement is, "I've fallen
in love with an American."

Her friends, of course, are amazed to hear this dignified,
happily married woman say such a thing. "Who is he?" they
gasp.

"I'll tell you later," she says evasively, and then politely
says goodbye and hangs up.

Naturally they call back with questions:

"Where did you meet him?"

"How old is he?"

"Does your husband know?"

Mrs. Ara happily answers all the questions. "We met in

San Francisco. . . . He's in his late eighties. . . . Yes, my husband knows about him. In fact, he's crazy about him, too."

Then she begins telling the caller about Dr. Shaklee and his philosophy. "Once they are sold on him," she explains, "and I feel they have trust and confidence in him, I tell about the products and the company. But I begin with Dr. Shaklee. I think it's important to let them know about Shaklee's heart and soul right from the beginning."

At the New Supervisors Convention Mrs. Ara vowed she would become a Coordinator in time to qualify for the following year's International Coordinators Convention in August 1978. She met her goals, and Mr. Ara joined her in Hawaii. For the Aras this trip was especially thrilling, since they had both lacked the energy before Shaklee nutrition to take any extensive trips. In Hawaii the couple made a commitment to a new goal: they would become Key Coordinators in time for the next ICC.

By November 1978 they had achieved their goal. Then they raised their sights. In August 1979, when they attained their new goal, they attended the ICC in Vienna as Master Coordinators. Although the Aras now rank among Shaklee's elite, they have remained modest about their position. "It is a great honor to be a Master," Mrs. Ara agrees, "but we shall always remember that we were simple Distributors in the beginning. Every morning I remind myself to keep my head from swelling, and not to think about the title and glamour that come with the position of Master." Today Mrs. Ara continues to sponsor new people into Shaklee, and she vows she always will. For her, sharing is the lifeblood of the business, and helping friends improve their health remains immensely satisfying.

The Ara organization, based in Kamakura, a city about fifty kilometers south of Tokyo, has expanded throughout Japan. The couple's twenty-four-year-old daughter is also employed in the business; in the true Shaklee tradition, the Aras' business has become a family enterprise. Mr. and Mrs. Ara also see their organization itself as a family. "We have only the one daughter," Mr. Ara reflects, "so we have wanted to have as many Supervisors as possible. They are like our children to us." His wife shares this feeling. At present, the Ara organization has twenty-one First Level Supervisors—a sizable family by any standard.

Although the Aras have never put monetary gain first, they have achieved considerable financial success in Shaklee. "I don't believe most of our people put financial gain first," Mrs. Ara says, "but even though a person may not be seeking a high income, it naturally follows if you share your Shaklee happiness." During the first half of 1981 the Aras' monthly bonus checks averaged 2,900,000 yen. At slightly above four dollars in U.S. currency per thousand yen, that's equivalent to an American monthly income of over $11,700! Although Mr. Ara holds a very good position, Japanese executives do not receive compensation of this size; through Shaklee the Aras have achieved financial ease beyond their wildest dreams. (The average annual income is higher in Japan than in the U.S. Nevertheless, the money they earn is just as impressive in Japan as it is here.)

Although U.S.-made products are respected and accepted by the Japanese, Mr. Ara is sometimes asked whether the nutritional needs of the Japanese are the same as those of Americans. "Of course they are," he says matter-of-factly. "People are people. The basic concept applies to all people everywhere." He does point out, however, that Japanese regulations have made certain product modifications necessary. Some of Shaklee's Japanese products, such as chewable Vita-Lea, taste slightly different. "Our taste in food is quite different from that of Americans," he says with a smile. "I doubt if the American Vita-Lea would be accepted in Japan. Likewise, Americans would probably not like the taste of our products."

Because Mr. Ara's position at NKK demands highly specialized knowledge, he has been granted special permission to work beyond the mandatory retirement age. At sixty-one, he realizes that the day must soon come when he will have to retire. When that happens, he will work full-time with his wife in Shaklee. "Shaklee has no mandatory retirement," he notes happily. "It is absolutely wonderful for a man who plans to join his wife after retiring. We stress this feature to Japanese couples. It gives a husband incentive to support his wife's career, because someday it will be his, too!" While Mr. Ara modestly describes himself as his wife's "assistant," Mrs. Ara is quick to point out that she often draws on his business experience; he also helps with the bookkeeping and, most important, lends his moral support.

The Aras have qualified for several bonus cars, although neither one of them has ever had a driver's license. The cars have been put to good use, however, since their daughter has used them to deliver Shaklee products. Conventions are another bonus the Aras enjoy. "Foreign trips are very special to us," Mr. Ara explains, his eyes twinkling with pleasure. "The Japanese are insatiable travelers. So we find this is a wonderful incentive for us to motivate our people."

Obviously, the Aras have found many benefits in Shaklee: foreign travel, bonus cars, financial security, and a huge new family. Of course, they also attribute their increased energy and good health to Shaklee products. But when asked what their greatest joy has been, Mrs. Ara replies that it's the thrill of sharing.

"We have an expression in Japan," she says, glowing with quiet happiness, "that goes, 'I can never sleep with my feet toward you.' In our country this is the highest compliment one can make, equivalent to saying, 'I can never repay you.' So often members of our Shaklee family come to us and say, 'I can never sleep with my feet toward you.' Nothing brings us more joy."

Acknowledgment: The author gratefully acknowledges Ryotaro Kanzaki, who served as translator during the interview with Mr. and Mrs. Ara.

10

❧ ❧

Think Big!
(*The Holker Story*)

ACHIEVING the rank of Shaklee Master Coordinator means reaching the highest position possible within the field organization, a position held by only a small fraction of all Shaklee people. To become a Master is tantamount to making baseball's Hall of Fame, or becoming one of the top money-earners on the PGA tour. To be the leading Master Coordinators, then, is a unique achievement. Kay and Bob Holker are at the top.

Because of their achievement, the Holkers have become near legends in direct selling. Who are they? And what makes them tick?

The house Bob and Kay live in is an expression of the family's unwritten rule: Think big! The house, inspired by a French castle, has seventy-six rooms and 40,000 square feet; it is reputed to be the largest home in Minnesota. The secluded nine-acre site includes orchards originally planted with specimens of the best apple trees from nearly every country in Europe, as well as plum trees, grape vines, and Kay's organic vegetable garden. Among its many other features, the house includes a separate guest house, thirteen bathrooms, and "about ten bedrooms." The house is so big that the Holkers had been in it three weeks when they discovered a full-sized room nobody had seen before. An estimated 50,000 people have come to Wayzata, a suburb of Minneapolis, to tour it.

The house is an excellent tool for recruiting people into Shaklee and motivating present members of the Holker organization. Tours of the home are given almost daily. Bob believes that the extra people the house has attracted to the Holker organization since the family moved in in 1973 have more than paid for the house. The Holker mansion is an unforgettable example of super success.

The Holkers have achieved financial success, but more important, they are a happy, healthy family. In their household, being a family means playing, singing, working, and praying together. They have the best of everything. Yet they are not content with the status quo. Growing is part of the Holker philosophy—reaching out and stretching. According to Bob Holker, you either go forward or backward, but there's no such thing as standing still.

The Holker philosophy has taken Kay and Bob a long way since they became Shaklee Distributors on November 25, 1963. The folks who live in the castle on the hill were then living in a small house trailer fifteen feet from a railroad track. Not only did the trains shake the little home when they passed, but at one point, rounding a bend, the engine headed directly for the trailer. At about that time "The Railroad Comes Through the Middle of the House" was a popular song, to their vast amusement. Kay hums a bar and says with a smile, "We were almost literally living that song!"

Like many young couples, Kay and Bob lived precariously on what Kay made. The $1.35 an hour she earned as a checkout girl in a discount store kept them in groceries while Bob went to college, where he majored in history and physical education, with the intention of becoming a coach. But despite the couple's relative poverty, they were not very interested in what Bob's older brother Tom had to say about Shaklee. Tom, a Distributor, wanted to sponsor them. Kay shrugged, and found an excuse to put him off.

Then, in November 1963, Tom's wife needed a ride to a meeting in Minneapolis, where Dr. Shaklee was to speak. Tom couldn't take her, and Kay didn't want to brave the winter weather alone, so Bob agreed to drive her.

Completely uninterested, Bob planned to remain in the car; but it became so cold that he decided to go in and see what was going on. The casual decision had electrifying results; Bob was so impressed by Dr. Shaklee's conviction and philosophy that he immediately made up his mind to become a Distributor. He left the meeting that night overflowing with enthusiasm.

When he told Kay about Dr. Shaklee's old-fashioned morality, so in tune with the Holkers' own Mormon beliefs, and about the opportunity in the company for a self-motivating couple, she was unimpressed. Even the description of the monthly bonus checks Bob had seen there, in amounts ranging up to $2,000, failed to move her. And she was least enthusiastic about Bob's sudden decision to quit college when he needed only thirteen credits to graduate.

"Who wouldn't be upset?" she asks today with a shrug. "I think if I'd been at the meeting I would have shared his enthusiasm from the start. But as it was . . ."

When Bob received his first bonus check in December, for $157, Kay was still not convinced that this had been the right decision. "In January," she explains, "he got his second check, for $652. And I started to think, Well, maybe there's something to this." In Bob's third month in the business, his wife became a believer; his February bonus check was more than her entire annual income.

The most amazing thing about this phenomenal beginning was that Bob was selling only one product, Basic-H. He simply didn't know much about the other Shaklee products. In his third month he had sold $33,000 worth of Basic-H.

Bob explains his success in terms of the high goals he set. Having no idea what his rate of achievement "ought to be," he decided to sponsor one person a day. "I just didn't know any better," the cheerful six-footer says with a grin. "I figured that somewhere, say out in California, there must be people who were sponsoring three, four, five people a day. Of course, nobody does that. Nobody sponsors one person a day, but I didn't know that. I figured one person a day was a modest goal, and since I was young and new in the business, that's what I set for myself." In his first month Bob sponsored twenty-five people. By the third month he and Kay had so much business they could hardly handle it.

From the beginning, Bob's approach was creative. One recruiting device he used involved his first bonus car, a Chevrolet Impala convertible with whitewall tires—"every college kid's dream car back then," he says. The day he took possession of the car, Bob drove it to the St. Cloud campus and parked it on the sidewalk at the entrance to the main library. On the windshield he placed a sign that read "This is a free Shaklee bonus car. Would you like one of these? If so, see Bob Holker downstairs in the library or call this number." Bob received numerous telephone calls later, but the real excitement took place in the library, where he gave presentations to so many students that he was finally asked to stand on a conference table so everyone could hear him. Between 200 and 300 students learned about Shaklee as a result of that day, and dozens were sponsored.

Within six months, the Holkers were among Shaklee's top money-makers. They became First Level Supervisors to Joan and Al Hegerman (since Bob's brother Tom had left Shaklee to become a district manager for the AAA Motor Club). One goal Kay and Bob set themselves was to make a million dollars for the Hegermans—and they've done it. "We feel very good about the money we've made for the Hegermans," Bob affirms. "After all, the more we make for them, the more we make for ourselves." Bob finds the fact that some people do not share this attitude disturbing. "They're being shortsighted. Instead of worrying about what the other guy is making off you—no matter what you do for a living—you should be grateful for how well you're doing. There's no room for petty jealousy in business."

When Bob was twenty-six and Kay twenty, they began to lose their enthusiasm for the business. "We were already at the top," Bob explains, "so I lost my motivation. I felt I had nowhere to go. The challenge was gone."

At the time, the restaurant business looked more challenging. Bob formed a partnership with his father, and the two began acquiring and operating drive-in restaurants. They eventually owned five. Bob poured his creativity into remodeling the buildings, redesigning menus, and insuring that good food was served. The partners also began operating miniature golf courses beside the drive-ins, with the idea that the drive-ins would bring business to the golf courses and vice versa.

Nearly three and a half years had passed when late one night Bob had a sudden realization.

"I'd put in twelve hours that day doing things that I could have paid some high school kid a dollar an hour to do. So my time was worth twelve dollars that day." Driving home, he continued to think about this fact. While the drive-in business was prospering, it didn't seem like a very profitable way to spend his time.

He was still thinking about this when he pulled up beside his darkened house, went in, and looked at the mail. The first envelope he opened was his Shaklee bonus check—for $2,200. "And I hadn't sponsored anybody for over three years!" he says. "I thought, 'I just worked twelve hours to earn twelve dollars. What would have happened if I'd spent that twelve hours working in the Shaklee business?' And I realized that I probably would have been able to develop a Supervisor."

During the same time period that Bob was thinking hard about his future, he received a phone call from Spokane. One of his closest friends, Lamont Nibarger, who had amassed a fortune building Rodeway Inns around the world, had an intriguing offer. He had just lost his right-hand man and wanted

Bob to move to Spokane and take the position—at $100,000 a year, which in 1968 seemed like all the money in the world to the Holkers.

"But I don't know the first thing about construction," Bob protested.

"That's okay. That's perfect. I'd rather you didn't know anything. I'll teach you to do things my way."

There was one other thing. Lamont would expect Bob to get out of Shaklee entirely so he could devote his full energies to the new job. Bob told him he'd have to think it over.

"I knew one thing right away," he says reflectively. "I was turned off when he said, 'I'll teach you to do things my way.'" An individualist to the core, Bob preferred to do things his own way.

Still, it was an attractive offer, and the decision, he knew, was a crucial one. The restaurant business was too demanding and kept him away from the family, but leaving it was a big step. The Shaklee business "came too easy; there didn't seem to be any challenge," but he thought he could make a great deal of money in it. And the job offer from Lamont, despite its drawbacks, was also appealing. Bob decided to find some solitude and search for an answer that felt right. Gathering up his sleeping bag and some books, he told Kay he was driving north to his favorite deer-hunting spot, an isolated area where there wasn't a single human being within a radius of twenty-five miles. He also told her that he intended to do without food or human companionship until he knew what to do. He would probably have an answer within a few hours, he thought.

"And I didn't get any answer at all that first night," he recalls. "I spent the night in the woods, listening to the wolves howl." The next morning, Bob was no closer to an answer. That night went by, and the next night, with no revelation. During this time he was getting lonely—and also very hungry.

On the third day, the answer came "like that!" Bob says, snapping his fingers. "And I knew it was the right answer."

He jumped in the jeep, drove home, and told Kay, "We're going to sell our miniature golf courses and our drive-in restaurants. I'm going to tell Lamont, 'No dice.' We're going with Shaklee full time."

Going full-time at this point in life was not easy for the Holkers, who were and still are very committed to working for the Mormon Church. Bob was a Sunday School superintendent and Kay was active in a young people's group. Both activities took many hours a week. But they were confident they would somehow find the time now that they knew their direction.

One way they did it was by "working smart." Bob believed that the only time that really counted in Shaklee was "prime time"—the hours between seven and ten at night, when meetings can be held. "What you do during the day is detail work, and basically not that important compared to the meetings," he says. By placing a high value on their time, the Holkers achieved astonishing results.

During the next thirty-seven month period, they held an average of four meetings a week (most Sales Leaders have traditionally held only one meeting a week). In that same period, Kay and Bob developed eighteen First Level Supervisors—an amazing feat, considering that throughout Shaklee's entire history only a handful of Masters have been able to develop more than eighteen First Levels, and that has taken them many years.

Using a business management approach, Kay and Bob delegated the work. Each was responsible for four or five supervisory groups at a given time. Once the group was formed, both would go to the group meetings for two weeks in a row. On the third week Kay would return alone to conduct a cosmetic class for the women. After that Kay and Bob would nurture the group along until it held its own weekly meetings. All groups also attended the Holkers' weekly meeting at their house.

Their house was no longer a trailer, but it was certainly

no mansion either. The meeting room was the traditional one for many beginners, the basement, which Kay and Bob "decorated" for the grand sum of $200. The money went on basics: paint for the walls and floor, curtains, and card-table chairs, accumulated a few at a time until they filled the room.

Then, as now, Holker meetings were broken into two parts. First Kay gave a presentation on the products; second, Bob talked about the business opportunity. Bob and Kay believe in always approaching a newcomer with the opportunity. "I realized," Bob explains, "that if I talked to a person only about the product, I might sell a quart of Basic-H and make sixty-one cents. But if I *sponsored* him . . . there was no comparison. What if we'd just been told about the product and ended up buying a quart of Basic-H? We've made the Hegermans over a million dollars. The person I'm introducing to Shaklee might do the same for me."

Bob is well aware that many people believe in selling the products first and, when product loyalty is established, then presenting the business opportunity. "First share with the guy and later talk business opportunity. Well, ever since we entered this business in 1963 we've talked business opportunity first. Without emphasizing the sharing.

"But look what happens! When we hold a meeting and people get turned on about the business opportunity, they don't just sign up to be Distributors just for their personal needs—they buy products by the case! It was common for our new Distributors to leave their first meeting with $200 worth of products, or sometimes $600 or $800 worth. But if we had talked about products only, we would have sold a small fraction of that."

The result of the Holker philosophy is that the Holker organization's annual sales run in excess of nine figures—more than many entire companies do in a year's time. "When you consider our sales volume, we've shared a great deal, haven't we?"

Bob and Kay also decided that their primary interest was

in bringing in breadwinners who might go full-time with Shak-lee. While many new Distributors must work up to a certain income level before they can do this, the Holkers also encourage ambitious people with the right talents to make an immediate full-time commitment.

In his speeches to his groups, Bob dilates upon how "all business opportunities are not created equal." He explains that in some fields considerable time and effort are demanded, but without the possibility of generous compensation. "But the return from Shaklee," he says earnestly, "is much greater for the time and effort you put into it than the return from just about anything else you could do. In my own case, the contrast between my restaurant earnings and our Shaklee business illustrates this." While Bob comes across as low-keyed, his sincerity and conviction show through as he says this; it's easy to see why his talks at meetings have galvanized his people into creating a thriving sales organization.

Bob Holker's unusual approach is typical of him; he is an individual who will not conform for the sake of conformity. He believes, in fact, that only nonconformists can be supersuc-cessful in today's world. "The person who really gets ahead is basically a dissenter," he says. "He creates his success and wealth by finding new and better ways. In fact, you *can't* make a million dollars today as a conformist. You've got to do your own thing. You've got to get a feeling from within and just follow it. Shaklee gives its people the freedom to do this."

One secret of Bob's success is his ambition. He has always set out to do more than anyone else would think possible. "Why not try to be number one?" he asks. "I feel everybody should have that goal, and we stress that to our children. Most people figure they're never going to get that far, so they just give up and settle for mediocrity. And if you're content to be average, that's all you'll ever be. But you know, it's even written on the walls of Congress, 'He aims too low who aims beneath the stars.'"

Kay interrupts gently: "It's not that being number one is so important; striving for it is what's important."

Bob nods. "That's right. The anticipation is really the best part. I've always wanted to be number one in whatever I was involved in. And in almost every case, once I've reached my goal I've felt a letdown. The striving, the hard work, that's what's so much fun."

One way the Holkers boost their own motivation is by announcing their ambitious goals. While some people feel embarrassed about having grand ideas, Bob is proud of his sky-high ambitions. "I write it down and then go and tell *everybody*," he proclaims. "I tell our people not to keep their goals a secret. Because I've found that once I let my friends and relatives and business associates know about my goals, I *have* to achieve them. It becomes a matter of pride. I'll do it because I don't want to lose face by not doing it."

While he talks, Kay is smiling fondly. "He likes to think big," she tells, "so our goals are high. We'll try to do more in a single year than most people try in ten years. But it's true, once we announce our goal, in Shaklee for instance, it's out there in front of a million people. So then we have to get on the ball and do it!"

The goals the Holkers set are always specific. Often a final goal is preceded by a number of specific short-term goals, but even these are apt to be so high they're unattainable. Some years ago Kay and Bob were told their goal of keeping their PV over $10,000 a month was unattainable.

"At that time nobody was doing $10,000 a month on a steady basis," Bob explains. "But we put forth an all-out effort, and for almost seven years we did $15,000 a month PV, month in and month out."

Typically, the Holkers were not content to rest on their laurels for long. Their next goal concerned their people who were doing $3,000 or $5,000 a month PV—a very respectable PV in most people's minds. The incentive the Holkers offered was simple: "We're going to have a fantastic dinner for every-body who gets their PV up to $10,000."

"Well," says Kay, "you wouldn't believe it! We had people come from all over the country, and we didn't even pay for their travel expenses, just the dinner."

The goal-setting also had a ripple effect. One of the Masters under the Holkers decided to have a $10,000 Club when she saw what they'd accomplished. As a result, she soon had many Supervisors in her group with over $10,000 a month PV.

Ultimately, the Holkers had forty-one people on their bo-nus recap who were doing over $10,000 a month. "Do you know what that does to your bonus check?" Kay asks with a winsome smile.

The Holkers have other examples of the power of thinking big. One woman in their organization learned to set high goals accidentally; intending to order 100 quarts of Basic-H, she received 100 cases instead. "Her husband almost died when he saw that semi pull up and unload those," Kay exclaims. "And then he just hit the ceiling. He didn't think they'd ever sell it, and he was hiding it under the beds and everywhere so nobody would know what a stupid thing she'd done. But the thing was, with all those cases of Basic-H he suddenly had a big goal to shoot for.

"He hadn't been very involved in her meetings up till that point, although he had been supportive. Now, though, he'd get up at every meeting and tell the people, 'This stuff comes in cases, and you have to buy it in cases if you want to sell a lot.' And before long every last case was sold. But if they hadn't had all those cases to sell, they would have still been selling one bottle at a time.

"It was a perfect example of the fact that you can be reach-ing a large goal in the same time it takes to reach a small one," Kay concludes.

Just before the Holker organization became the top organi-zation in Shaklee, Bob and Kay set the goal of being number one. To announce that goal and keep it in the forefront of everyone's mind, Bob bought gold necklaces with "#1" pendants for Kay and all of their First Level Sales Leaders.

Now that the Holkers are number one in Shaklee, Kay wears a different necklace—a tiny gold Rolls-Royce. Bob confirms that their next goal is a Shaklee bonus Rolls-Royce. At the 1981 International Coordinators Convention, the company gave Masters like the Holkers a new goal by announcing that Master Coordinators who had twenty-two Sales Leaders, of whom eleven are Coordinators on their First Level, would be entitled to his-and-her matching Cadillacs or Lincoln Continentals, as well as an extra ½ percent on their monthly bonus checks. Bob and Kay are aiming higher, however, for another added incentive offers a Rolls-Royce, as well as another additional ½ percent, to any Master with thirty Sales Leaders, of whom fifteen are Coordinators. It is typical of the Holkers to shoot straight for the Rolls-Royce.

Not so incidentally, this achievement would mean another substantial boost in the Holkers' income. According to Bob, the 1 percent bonus increase could mean an extra $25,000 a month on their bonus check. Is it the money or the challenge that motivates Kay and Bob? Perhaps not even they know the answer to that one for sure.

However goal-oriented the Holkers may be in their business, they are not the kind of achievers who are obsessed with material success. In fact, their family lifestyle has remarkable balance. Bob explains that his own philosophy stresses the three dimensions of life—physical, mental, and spiritual. "When I was very young," he says, "I realized that not many people put the same effort into all three facets of life. I became determined that I would, though, and I always have. Kay and I want our children brought up to be healthy in all three ways."

The Holkers' emphasis on physical well-being is perhaps most obvious. Six of their seven children are involved in sports (the seventh is only eighteen months old). The family plays basketball together in a regulation college-sized indoor basketball court which Bob had built onto their home. The court is in their sports complex, which includes a professional handball/racquetball court, men's and women's dressing rooms, a deluxe exercise room with up-to-date training equipment, and a sauna. The basketball court is marked so it can also be used for indoor tennis and volleyball.

Running is another major family sport. Bob, of course, had already run thousands of miles by the time he and Kay married. She was his first convert within the family. She enjoys telling about how long it took to sell her on the idea.

"I grew up on a farm," she explains, "and I rode horses, but there weren't any girls' sports in those days. Then when we'd been married several years Bob said to me, 'Okay honey, you've got to start running.'

"I said, 'Running? Forget it. I'm not going to run!' Back in those days nobody ran, let alone girls.

"Well, he just kept on running himself every morning, going around the track at the high school near us. Pretty soon he convinced me to try it. I sort of liked it, but I was embarrassed because I'd die after a short distance, so I'd run after dark, and he'd go ahead on his bike to keep away the dogs."

Before long Kay was up to three miles a day and running the high school track in the morning with Bob, while the baby sat on the grass and Tami, then a preschooler, ran alongside.

"And that's how the children learned to run," Kay concludes. "As each one got old enough, he or she wanted to join us and run too." The power of this example is obvious in the Holker family. Tami, now a college freshman, won the state championship for the 3,000-meter run; some track observers believe she can be the national collegiate champion in the event.

"There are three ways to lead—or to teach kids," Bob summarizes. "Number one, by example; number two, by example; and number three, by example. That's why we believe in having a high PV, because it sets an example for the people in our organization. If we can do it, they can do it too."

As the Holker children grow, it is increasingly clear that their parents' example is having its effect. Just as Bob and Kay believe in setting high goals for themselves, they have taught their children to aim for the top. Kay says, "We want our kids to believe they can do anything they try to do."

Marty Holker, twelve years old, has already aimed his sights high. A star basketball player in his age group, he has a simple goal: to be the best basketball player in the world. "And if he wants to badly enough, he'll do it," Bob says. "I think it's very healthy for him to have such a clear, ambitious goal. And he knows that it will take a lot of work, but all he has to do is get out there and do it."

Each of the Holker children is growing up with the philosophy of aiming high. "As far as I'm concerned," Bob says earnestly, "they shouldn't just aim to win a gold medal in the Olympics. They should aim to do it in their event in the fastest time ever recorded. After all, if you shoot for the stars and don't make it, so what? But shoot for the stars!"

Kay and Bob believe that a commitment to athletics enriches their children in many ways. "They learn to set personal goals for themselves," Bob explains. "And they learn that it requires a great deal of discipline to excel. They also learn to pick themselves up after they lose and try again. Take two boxers fighting for the championship of the world. One of them has to lose. And that's true in every sport. It's like life. You've got to be able to take defeat without being defeated. You've got to figure out how to come back and be stronger the next time."

Far from feeling pressured by this emphasis on winning, the Holker children enjoy sports. "Some people think we put too much pressure on them to achieve," Bob says, "but we're right out there running beside them, playing basketball with them, and that's different. I've probably run 10,000 miles with Tami. It's *fun*. Our kids would rather come home and play basketball with the family than go to the movies."

In the physical-mental-spiritual balance that the Holkers strive to achieve, family singing plays an important part. Originally the Holkers began singing together for their own entertainment. Later they found themselves being asked to sing at Shaklee rallies and conventions all over the country. Now they practice on their own stage, which is fully equipped with a sophisticated sound system. Their performances have been so well received that recently they appeared at the University of Minnesota in concert with Bob Hope. The performances have given the children considerable stage presence and confidence, but Bob is proudest of the way music has taught them to work together.

"Working Together as a Shaklee Family" is one of Bob's favorite subjects; at the 1976 ICC in Acapulco he spoke on this theme. At the close of his speech about how his own family pulls together, Kay and the children came marching down the aisle and onstage singing, "Pulling Together, We Can Work It Out." The tearful audience gave the singing Holkers a standing ovation.

As Kay and Bob talk about their children, it becomes obvious that they are devoted parents. Bob enjoys his freedom within Shaklee to take time with his children when it is most meaningful. Last year he attended 114 basketball games in which the children played. He also likes to come home in midafternoon and play a pick-up game with them before going back to his work.

For Kay, the freedom to be with the children has been tremendously important. "Where else can you have this kind of time?" she asks. "I feel sorry for all those women who are working mothers and have to work nine to five every day. That just isn't the best way to raise a family."

Motivation by example is probably the key to the Holkers' success. One of Bob's favorite sayings is, *"Success in Shaklee is not in finding the right person, but in being the right person."* Both he and Kay practice as well as preach. They believe that living the Shaklee philosophy is the only sure way to success.

As Bob says, "In this business you're a hypocrite if you go around smoking and drinking and you're thirty pounds overweight. You can't carouse half the night and then stand up the next day in front of a group of Shaklee people telling them about good health! To be supersuccessful in Shaklee, you've got to be in top physical condition; and you've also got to get yourself straight spiritually and mentally. When you do, the recruiting is automatic." The proof of that statement is in the fact that almost daily the Holkers receive calls and letters from people *asking* to be sponsored by them.

Obviously, Bob and Kay are in total agreement with the Shaklee philosophy, which is undoubtedly a major reason for their astonishing success. "Our priorities are God first, family second, and career third," Kay says softly. "This is the same philosophy we held before Shaklee, and tried to live by all our lives. It's so good to be with a company that believes as we do."

Bob credits their success to something else, too: the American free enterprise system. "The opportunity in Shaklee exemplifies American free enterprise," he says. "Look at almost any large company and you'll see that the system is not programmed for supersuccess. It's programmed against it. You can only go so high. But Shaklee isn't like that at all." He pauses thoughtfully and then concludes, "Shaklee really is what American free enterprise ought to be; it offers each individual an opportunity to dare to be different."

11

The Sharing and Caring Corporation

OVER A HUNDRED YEARS AGO, Henry David Thoreau said, "It is true enough that a corporation has no conscience; but a corporation of conscientious men is a corporation with a conscience." Shaklee was founded as a company with a conscience. Although there have been many changes since 1956—in products, people, and location—this philosophy has never wavered.

Today the company's founders are retired from active management (although Forrest and Lee remain on the Board of Directors) but the original philosophy is still actively practiced. Shaklee's CEO, Gary Shansby, says, "This company practices the Golden Rule day in, day out, both here at the home office and in the field. That philosophy is part of Shaklee's heritage, and we take great pride in it."

While previous chapters have illustrated the company's sincere caring for its sales force, Shaklee's dedication to practicing the Golden Rule is also evident in the thoughtfulness it extends to home-office employees. The company's commitment to treating employees well is so widely known that there is a waiting list of applicants at every facility.

One of the best-known and most unusual fringe benefits

the company offers is its Centerra at Shaklee Terraces, the corporate headquarters. This unique physical-fitness facility occupies the third floor of the building. It includes the most modern exercise equipment as well as a 230-foot track. On his first visit to Centerra, an employee is given an orientation session, physiological tests, and a personal exercise program to follow. After each workout, employees take their exercising pulse rates, and this information is recorded by a computer so that progress can be measured. Two full-time professionals are on hand to advise and instruct all participants. Each employee also receives, at no charge, a locker and workout clothes. At the end of the session, he drops his workout outfit in a bin; it is laundered that evening and ready again the next morning.

Centerra occupies 14,000 square feet in an area of San Francisco where office space costs about forty dollars a square foot. Moreover, the annual cost of the program is estimated to be $700 per employee. How does the company justify providing this facility? The answer, of course, is that healthy people are more productive on the job. Turnover and absenteeism are reduced, and morale is higher. "It works!" says Gary Shansby with a smile. Shaklee's personable CEO is himself a devout physical-fitness enthusiast; he runs several miles every day.

Shaklee Terraces also includes a restaurant, the Cafe Terra. This cafeteria attracts the general public and gives Shaklee employees a 20 percent discount.

Each Shaklee floor has a fruit juice and vitamin bar where employees can have free juice and food supplements. Shaklee employees are encouraged to take health breaks at these bars rather than the customary coffee and cigarette breaks. As a consequence, there are few smokers at the home office. For those who do smoke, the company recently offered a series of eight-week quit-smoking courses conducted by Smokenders. This course cost $200, with the employee and the company each paying half. For added incentive, the company paid each employee fifty dollars if he was still not smoking three months later, and another fifty dollars after three more months. Thus, for participants who successfully stayed off cigarettes for six months the program was free. At the end of the six months each quitter was presented with a certificate; Gary Shansby personally made the presentations.

Shaklee's interest in the health and well-being of employees has been expressed in a Fitness Day. Employees demonstrate their pledges to fitness in a series of sporting events, including five-kilometer and ten-kilometer foot races, ten- and twenty-mile cycling events, and a 2.5-mile walking event. Departments compete vigorously in team events, such as tug-of-war, softball, and volleyball. There's no question that Shaklee Fitness Day is a far cry from the typical company picnic!

Consideration of employees' well-being is not just an extracurricular matter at Shaklee but extends into the working day itself. One successful innovation at the home office is flextime, a system which allows employees to work their own hours, limited only by the requirements of their jobs and specific core hours. Within the hours from seven to six-thirty, each employee chooses the work schedule that fits him best. In this way, office people can create time for physical fitness, community and civic activities, and other outside interests.

At the Norman, Oklahoma, plant, under another innovative work system, the majority of employees are organized into work teams. Depending on the nature of their jobs, the teams have from three to fifteen members. Each team selects its own work hours, sets it own production schedule, selects new team members, and even initiates employee discharges when necessary. Employees enjoy a high degree of autonomy within this system. As one Norman worker said, "It's as if you owned a job rather than worked for somebody. It gives you a sense of pride and makes you want to always do your best." Plant manager Larry Clark notes that work teams give employees the opportunity to be independent and self-motivated. "If you're treated fairly," he adds, "you'll be more productive. So far the team concept has been very successful for us."

Another way Shaklee shows that it cares about its people is through its semi-annual meetings, at which employees have an opportunity to talk with top management. For one of its recent town hall–type meetings Shaklee bused employees to Davies Symphony Hall, where Gary Shansby and other executives opened the floor to questions and comments. These meetings not only involve employees in the management process, but also serve as a forum for giving awards for special achievement.

Shaklee people are proud to belong to a company that lives its philosophy, and Shaklee's caring and sharing is no family secret. The word is out, in San Francisco at least; executives from other companies have been known to say things like "Your people are spoiled, and *our* people are griping. They want to know when we're going to do for them what you do for your employees."

Shaklee's good will for others extends well beyond caring for its own people. As a fine corporate citizen, Shaklee supports numerous charitable and civic organizations.

There are thousands of worthy causes, and it is obviously impossible for any institution to support all of them. Furthermore, the federal government limits a corporation's deductions on its donations of its pre-tax income. Therefore, Shaklee management has developed certain criteria for the company's charitable contributions. Claude Jarman, Vice President of Corporate Communications, explains: "Our preference is to support causes which uphold our philosophy and have some relationship to our company. For example, we're concerned about good health, and it's natural for us to be more interested in preventive medicine than curative medicine."

Shaklee's favorite causes often fit the company's philosophy in more than one way. The U.S. Ski Team is a good example. In November 1980, the company made a commitment to be "Official Nutrition Consultant" to the United States Ski Team through the 1984 Olympics. The company will provide its expertise in nutritional programs, supply food supplements, and support training and competition for the national Alpine and Nordic ski teams. This contribution is particularly well received, since the U.S. Ski Team is one of only two national ski teams in the world that is not supported by government funding. Shaklee's belief in good health and well-being is well represented in this support of athletic activities and physical fitness.

Other sports activities Shaklee has supported include the United States Davis Cup Team and the Transamerica Tennis Tournament. The Davis Cup Team, a non-profit venture, requires financial support from the private sector. Commenting on this type of philanthropy, Gary Shansby says he believes that corporations can spend money more wisely than government bureaucracies. He adds that charitable contributions like these are not given away or wasted but *invested,* and "investment in society is good insurance for the free enterprise system."

The Special Olympics Winter Games is another favorite cause of Shaklee's. These Special Olympics, originally started by Robert Kennedy, allow mentally handicapped youngsters of all ages to participate in winter sports. Claude explains that "most of them have never before had an opportunity to ski. In fact, many have never even seen snow." In the two long weeks of the San Francisco 1982 Special Olympics at Lake Tahoe, more than 130 young people competed. Although they are encouraged to experience the joy of competition, the emphasis in the Special Olympics is not on winning but on participating.

Claude points out that the company has a strong commitment to lending its support to the communities which most affect the company, "those where we have our facilities and major sales activity. We believe it's our duty to be involved in the community." Like many major corporations, Shaklee is aware of its responsibility to the local community, and of the importance of making sure San Francisco will always be capable of attracting and retaining good people in the competitive employment market. Shaklee demonstrated its commitment to the City of San Francisco when, in 1980, it moved into its present headquarters. At a time when some companies were leaving the downtown area, Shaklee Terraces was an architectural statement of the company's faith in the city. Since then, Shaklee has remained committed to San Francisco, particularly in its support of the city's famed cultural life.

One of the many philanthropic gestures Shaklee has made in the city began over a lunch table several years ago. Gary Shansby and George Moscone, then Mayor of San Francisco, had been talking about Proposition 13.

"It's really hurting us," the Mayor lamented. "All sorts of things are being cut. Take the Golden Gate Park Band. They've been playing free concerts in the park every Sunday for over fifty years. Now we just can't keep them."

"What would it cost to keep them?" Gary asked.

The Mayor promised to let him know.

As a result of the conversation, Shaklee pledged to finance the concerts one month a year for two years. Furthermore, Gary spoke to other executives until eleven more companies were persuaded to support the band year-round.

Although, as Gary is the first to point out, Shaklee's contribution was not a major one in financial terms—about $5,000— it saved a San Francisco tradition. "As a company," he adds, "we felt very good about how we'd been able to help out."

Shaklee's generosity has been particularly evident in its support of the arts. When the King Tut exhibit came to town in 1979, Shaklee was a major supporter. In 1981 the company went a step further and became the sole sponsor of an exhibit displaying 300 objects designed by the American painter and stained-glass artist, Louis Comfort Tiffany. This was the first major showing of Tiffany's work, and the first time any corporation had fully underwritten a major exhibition at the city's magnificent M. H. de Young Museum. The art of Tiffany, one of America's great artists, had long been out of fashion, but the critical and public response to the Tiffany show was over-whelming. While more people saw the King Tut exhibit, the number of people per hour who visited the Tiffany show was the largest in San Francisco's history.

For Shaklee's generosity in supporting both exhibits, the museum scheduled special times for each exhibit to be open exclusively to Shaklee people. During the 1981 ICC, thousands of Shaklee people viewed the Tiffany collection.

Shaklee also generously supports public television in the San Francisco area. In 1980 the company helped underwrite the MacNeil/Lehrer Report, an in-depth news program that has won the Emmy, the Peabody, and the DuPont/Columbia awards. In 1981 Shaklee sponsored a film documentary on Ansel Adams, world-famous nature photographer. Adams's commitment to nature, of course, fits the Shaklee philosophy, and he is a good friend of the company. Photographs by him are included in the art that adorns the home office.

Community support is evident at other Shaklee locations as well. Like Shaklee Terraces, the plant at Norman, Okla-homa, is a showplace that fits into and enhances the commu-nity. In keeping with Shaklee's "close to nature" concept, the Norman plant has a low profile and is nestled in the woods and hills. "We didn't want to disturb anything," plant director Larry Clark says. "For instance, we've never exercised the zoning variance we obtained to put up a larger sign." The plant, which is across from the University of Oklahoma, is so well designed that many people mistake it for part of the campus. One interesting way the company gives to the Nor-man community is through its one-mile Parcourse, where Shaklee employees and the public can jog and exercise at no charge.

Both by example and by incentive, Shaklee encourages its employees to care and share, too. For instance, the com-pany matches two-for-one employee gifts to colleges, universi-ties, the U.S. Olympic Committee, and organizations promot-ing the arts and health and physical fitness.

Employees give thousands of hours each year to various

charitable causes. While there is no company policy giving employees the right to do volunteer work on company time, individual department heads have the discretion to permit this paid time-off, and many do. In some cases, volunteer work is done partly on the employee's time and partly on the company's time. For the company-sponsored Special Winter Olympics, many employees worked on company time to go to the Sierras and help with the project.

When it comes to individual charitable efforts, Shaklee's top executives lead by example. Gary Shansby maintains a high profile in the community as chairman of the San Francisco Chamber of Commerce and chairman of the Republican Party in Northern California. In addition, he serves on the boards of several civic organizations and governmental commissions. Claude Jarman is President of the Board of Trustees of the War Memorial and Performing Arts Center in San Francisco, and a national trustee of the Washington Opera in Washington, D.C. One of the company's young executives is President of the San Francisco Junior Chamber of Commerce, and another chairs the California Commission on Food and Nutrition. Similarly, an executive at the Norman facility serves on the advisory task force to the Oklahoma Governor's Council on Fitness and Health. While it would take too long to list all the philanthropic activities Shaklee people participate in, these examples illustrate the commitment and involvement of the company's executives.

The people at the Norman plant are equally involved in their community and in work on numerous local projects. Shaklee employees there have contributed time and money to the United Way Drive, the restoration of the historic Sooner Theatre, the Huston Huffman Physical Fitness Center at the University, the Chamber of Commerce, the Red Cross, and many other causes.

If these examples inspire other Shaklee people to volunteer their time to a cause, they can find their niches through SERVE—Shaklee Employees Resource Volunteer Effort.

SERVE works to match the right person with the right organization. In some cases, SERVE organizes group projects, such as a reforestation program at Golden Gate Park, during which Shaklee volunteers donated time and energy planting trees.

As a philanthropic company, Shaklee has focused primarily on local causes. It has also, however, contributed generously to the needy in faraway places.

One major effort in 1980 came about in response to a letter a Distributor sent to Gary Shansby. The problems the letter detailed were familiar to Gary; as a result of war and civil disruption, millions of Cambodians were facing starvation. "Is there anything the company can do to help?" the writer asked.

Gary took the letter to Dr. James Scala, Shaklee's Vice President of Science and Technology, who immediately advised donating some Vita-Lea. "This would be given to children," he explained, "and they need the calcium in Vita-Lea." The fact that the product was chewable meant that it would be easy to use by children who had never taken pills before. Soon thereafter, Shaklee sent 38 million Vita-Lea vitamin and mineral tablets to Cambodia. The shipment, which weighed 130,000 pounds, cost $60,000 to ship by air, and represented approximately $1 million worth of products.

Shaklee donates a considerable amount of time and money to various causes. How does the sales force react to the idea of so much being given away?

"They love it," Claude Jarman concludes. "They know that everything we do reinforces the Shaklee philosophy. And many have expressed their pride in being associated with a company that has a conscience. They don't want us to just say we care—they want us to show it."

12

Where Nature and Know-How Join Hands

"IF WE ARE GOING TO ENJOY our lives and reach our fullest potential," Gary Shansby says, "we must be in good health—both mentally and physically.

"There's been a lot written about the effect of mental health on physical health. The two are inseparable. Worry, stress, fear—the whole gamut of emotional problems—can play havoc with an otherwise healthy body. We are all aware of the seriousness of psychosomatic illnesses, and as a result the popularity of 'pop' psychology books and tapes is at an all-time high. Today more people than ever are enrolling in courses to improve their mental attitudes and reduce the stress in their lives—transactional analysis, assertiveness training, meditation, the list goes on and on.

"People today are also aware of the need for a personal physical fitness program. Just look around you and you'll see people engaged in all sorts of exercise—jogging, tennis, aerobic dancing, and calisthenics at health spas. And look at the general public concern about other health issues, such as smoking and overweight. Month after month, there's at least one weight-loss book on the best-seller lists.

"It's wonderful that Americans are actively doing so much

to improve their health," Gary stresses. "However, there's one major area that's still frequently neglected—nutrition. Many people suffer from nutritional deficiencies. It's easy to see why. Nobody is out there campaigning against positive thinking or physical fitness, but billions of dollars are spent every year to advertise junk foods and entice people to eat poorly. Consequently, most American diets are nutritionally inadequate.

"You've got to supply your body with the fuel it needs to keep it working smoothly. Personally, I believe that the only way you can be certain you're getting good nutrition is to take food supplements. I have friends who thought they had good diets and finally decided to try supplements, and they felt better. It makes a real difference.

"Here at Shaklee," Gary continues, "we think of ourselves as having a mission to help people get everything they possibly can out of life. Nutrition is one of the key elements that contribute to an individual's *total* well-being. This is our primary focus."

Dr. James Scala, Vice President of Science and Technology, and a nationally recognized nutrition expert, agrees. "What Gary is describing is optimum health—the ability to be all that you can be. And the foundation of optimum health is clearly optimum nutrition."

Jim Scala also points out that, although there is a growing public awareness of the need for good nutrition, most people don't know how to fill that need. "Taste and convenience dictate our eating habits," he states. "Furthermore, we've been programmed to overcook our foods, which decreases nutritional value, and to use too much discretionary sugar and salt on what we eat. The American way of life compounds the problem—we're exposed to far too many convenience foods, processed foods, and junk foods. We're also eating more and more meals in restaurants, where it's difficult to know what ingredients are in a dish, how fresh they are, and how they've been processed. The end result of all this is that even a person who knows a great deal about nutrition is hard-pressed to eat three balanced meals a day."

One major problem in the American diet began to appear in 1870, when processed foods first became available. Since 1900, processing methods have caused the crude fiber in the average American's diet to drop by about 50 percent. Fiber—found in whole grains, fresh fruits, and fresh vegetables—plays a vital function in the diet by *not* being digested. Instead, it passes through the system unchanged, adding important bulk during the digestive process and contributing to regularity. It also seems likely that inadequate fiber plays a major role in weight increase. But, although many people have become aware of the importance of fiber in recent years, it seems unlikely that America will ever return to a diet based on fresh farm produce and unprocessed grains and cereals.

While fiber has decreased in the American diet, fat has increased. Jim Scala refers to 1933 as "the cut-off point—the year America stopped eating a prudent diet. That year the fat intake of the average American rose to over 30 percent of his total caloric intake. And now it's slightly over 40 percent." The sugar intake of the average American has similarly increased, from below 100 pounds a year to 129 pounds a year, a 30 percent increase. Oddly enough, discretionary sugar—what you put in your coffee and tea and on your breakfast cereal—has actually decreased by about 50 percent in recent years. Jim's explanation is that "people know they should be eating less sugar, but we're eating it without seeing it! We're living in a sea of sugar. We're eating sugar in such foods as lunch meats and canned foods and we don't even know it. They're even adding sugar to the salt at some of the fast-food restaurants. I repeat, we're eating it without seeing it."

Fast-food restaurants, like packaged convenience foods, are responsible for other important changes in the American diet. Jim explains that the basic four food groups (meat and fish, grains and cereals, dairy products, and fruits and vegetables) have now been joined by a fifth group: highly processed foods. This group includes foods that are high in fats, sweets, and alcohol, and often high in calories but low in nutrients. These popular foods include pretzels, potato chips, soft drinks, candy bars, sugar-coated cereals, french fries, and other deep-fried fast foods. Despite their high fat, sugar, and calorie content, these foods are often consumed in excessive amounts, so that there is no room in the diet for more nutritious foods.

Another change in the American diet is a decrease in the consumption of milk. "Our favorite national beverage for children and young adults has changed from milk to soft drinks," he says. "As a result, we have a widespread calcium problem, which, unfortunately, is not widely recognized. Most women, for instance, need four glasses of milk a day to meet their calcium needs, but typically drink almost no milk because of their desire to control their weight and their cholesterol levels. I think women are more aware of inadequate iron in their diets, which is very widespread, than they are of inadequate calcium intake. In any case, the effects of a calcium-deficient diet won't even show up for many years. But the body's need for calcium is so critical that the body will actually leach it out of the bones to get the amount it needs if the diet doesn't supply it. The consequence, of course, shows up in old age: brittle bones that break easily in the elderly."

The desire to lose weight leads many Americans into unsound diets. While the average American does not get the U.S. Recommended Daily Allowance (RDA) of some nutrients, fad diets simply compound the problem. For instance, many dieters eliminate fats from the diet, although the calories from fats are not more fattening than calories from any other source, and fatty acids are needed to perform vital functions in the body. Dieters who cut back too far on dairy products often reduce the level of minerals needed to maintain strong bones and teeth. The most conscientious dieter will find it difficult to consume adequate nutrients through food alone once the intake drops below 2,500 calories.

"Under 2,000 calories," Jim says, "it's just about impossible to get what you need from your food. And I would estimate that about 50 percent of all American women take in fewer than 2,000 calories a day. Government surveys show an average intake of around 1,500 calories, and it's extremely difficult to get adequate amounts of all nutrients at this level—even for a nutritionist."

Modern nutrition has also been affected by drugs, which act in various ways to impair nutrition. Some drugs tend to speed up the excretion of nutrients before they can be absorbed. Others may interfere with the body's ability to convert nutrients into usable form. There are about 10,000 drugs on the market, and the action of many of them is not understood. Each drug, however, has a nutritional impact. Birth-control pills, for example, lower the blood levels of certain vitamins, notably folic acid and vitamin B-6, as well as several minerals. Anti-convulsants used to control epilepsy increase the turnover rate of vitamin D and folic acid. Many non-prescription drugs affect nutrition as well, including diuretics, antacids, and laxatives. Over a period of time, drug-induced depletion of specific nutrients can result in serious problems.

The use of cigarettes and alcohol also affects the body's nutrient requirements. Carbon monoxide and carbon dioxide, which enter the blood stream as a result of smoking, seem to have the ability to react with vitamin C and destroy it. Likewise, alcohol can cause the symptoms of B-vitamin deficiency in heavy drinkers and alcoholics. Jim explains that the body metabolizes the alcohol—which has calories but few nutrients—in preference to other substances in order to prevent the alcohol from going to the brain, where it impairs the ability to function. "It's a situation where the body protects itself at the expense of something else," he says. "Other parts of the metabolism stop, and certain B vitamins begin to build up—but the vitamins are shunted aside and not used. Consequently, the individual shows symptoms of deficiency. Then the body starts to synthesize fat in an attempt to regenerate those vitamins, and the fat is deposited on the liver. When the body builds scar tissue around the fat, that's cirrhosis. And some of this damage can be avoided by the simple addition of more of the B vitamins. Obviously, however, the best solution is to quit drinking; but for those who don't quit, taking vitamins can be a significant help."

Changes in the American lifestyle have also adversely affected our nutrition. One striking example is the modern habit of skipping breakfast. Many people do so because the traditional heavy breakfast of bacon, eggs, toast, and juice has gained a bad reputation among people who are conscious of cholesterol. But research clearly indicates that mental and muscular efficiency are lowest in the morning. "And they will remain low," Jim Scala adds, "unless there is a meal—in spite of the apparent lift that comes from a cup of coffee." Studies of the performance of athletes and schoolchildren have verified this; groups that have eaten well-balanced breakfasts do significantly better than those that have not. Dietary analyses reveal that for those who dislike eating traditional breakfast foods there are numerous nutritious alternatives. A glass of milk with vegetable protein powder, a favorite among Shaklee people, is actually more nutritious than the standard breakfast mentioned above.

One of the subtlest influences on modern nutrition is stress. "Stress," as scientists use the term, does not necessarily result from negative events or emotions. It can occur from hearing good news or bad news, from stage fright, busy traffic, a slow elevator, or an upcoming wedding in the family. Stress is so inevitable that it's even stressful to try to avoid it!

According to Jim, a classic study of the physiological impact of stress has been observed in racing car drivers. "Many physiological changes take place in the driver before the race actually begins. These changes occur because the body *knows* what's about to happen, and the hormones begin to react. Adrenaline is pumped into the system, the liver mobilizes glycogen to rush to the muscles. He's ready for anything. It's the 'fight or flight' syndrome. The survival of primitive man depended on his ability to mobilize all his resources like this. As a result, certain parts of the metabolism will go from resting levels to levels elevated 10,000 times or more."

The effects of stress on the body's nutritional needs are complex and difficult to predict. Research has established that the B-complex vitamins, zinc, and usually vitamins C and E are involved. Stress also affects the body's endocrine, nervous, and immunological systems, but individual reactions vary widely. While no one can avoid stress altogether, well-nourished, healthy people are unquestionably better equipped to handle it.

Jim points out that it is not always desirable to avoid stress, although it is desirable to be aware of its effect on nutritional needs. "An athlete in training, for instance, exercises his body day after day so he'll be equal to the stress of the event," he observes. "Interestingly enough, that athlete's needs for nutrition seems to increase disproportionately. You would think that if he burns 4,000 calories a day, he needs twice as many nutrients as the person who burns 2,000—but that may not be true. There's some evidence that the nutritional requirements increase in disproportion, and he may need the nutritional equivalent of 5,000 calories."

The amount of nutrients an individual needs varies not only with stress but with age. For instance, during the years of greatest growth (ages eleven through fourteen for girls, and thirteen through sixteen for boys), teenagers have higher nutrient needs than either younger children or adults. Unfortunately, the diet of the American teenager tends to be even worse than that of his parents. Food is often used to express independence from the parents when the youngster refuses more nourishing family food in favor of junk food. Since eating is an integral part of the teenage social scene, many teenagers consume an abundance of fast foods and snacks that are low in nutritional value.

Elderly Americans often show nutritional deficiencies, too.

Although an elderly person's health is, in a sense, the result of a lifetime of food habits, it's never too late to improve health. Studies in geriatric institutions show that carefully planned diets lead to increased appetites, weight gains, better sleep, and more interest in outside activities. One problem affecting the nutritional status of the elderly is that the metabolism slows down with age and fewer calories are needed, but there is no corresponding decrease in the need for vitamins and minerals. Numerous other factors affect the nutrition of the elderly, as well, including the increased cost of food, poor access to shopping, fading vision so that following recipes is difficult, loss of appetite due to loneliness and depression, and inability to chew food well. The diets of the elderly are often found to be inadequate in calories, protein, iron, vitamin A, vitamin C, and calcium. "Food supplements are an ideal way to improve nutritional status," Jim notes. "They're simple to use and inexpensive."

A 1980 survey conducted by the U.S. Department of Agriculture found that most Americans at all ages and income levels were not consuming the RDA of some essential vitamins and minerals. As previously pointed out, it is extremely difficult for the average person in today's fast-paced society to maintain a well-balanced diet. Furthermore, exact nutritional requirements are determined by all the thousands of differences that make each human being unique. There is no magic formula for a perfect nutritional program that can be applied to everybody. Age, amount of exercise, diet, occupation, stress, lifestyle, and numerous other factors determine individual needs. An infant, a professional athlete, a pregnant woman, a smoker, a woman on a weight-loss diet, and a heavy drinker all have different nutritional requirements.

When Shaklee was founded in 1956, Dr. Shaklee made a commitment to work toward meeting the nutritional needs of all people. In the early days of the company, all research and product development was conducted by Dr. Shaklee himself. Today, the Forrest C. Shaklee Research Center in Hayward, California, has one hundred people on its staff. Of these, seventy have bachelors' degrees or better, including seven who have Ph.D.'s in various scientific disciplines. The Research Center itself has twice as many scientists as that of any other nutritional products company.

Jim Scala manages all aspects of corporate research and development, and supervises nutritional programs and quality assurance at the Hayward facility. Jim is widely recognized as a leading expert in the field of nutrition and is listed in *Who's Who in America.* He joined Shaklee in 1978 as Vice President of Science and Technology, because "the company stood for everything I've practiced all my life. Furthermore, Shaklee is in the heart of nutrition, working on some of the really vital issues. The company's philosophy of harmony with Nature and its concern about personal health are completely compatible with my own beliefs. Perhaps the most exciting and rewarding times of my career have been the hours my staff and I have spent exchanging ideas and philosophies with Dr. Shaklee."

After graduating from Columbia in 1960, Jim went on to Cornell, where he earned a Ph.D. in biochemistry in 1964. He was hired by Owens-Illinois, where he started a life sciences research program. In 1971 he joined the Lipton Company as Director of Nutrition, and in 1975 he became Director of Nutrition and Health Sciences at General Foods, which has one of the largest nutrition research departments in the United States.

Presently he serves as a lecturer at Georgetown University School of Medicine and Dentistry and teaches a course in nutrition at the University of California, Berkeley. He has also conducted graduate programs in biochemistry at the University of Toledo and the Ohio College of Medicine. He is active in government organizations and foundations relating to nutrition, and is on the Board of Trustees of the Nutrition Foundation. His professional affiliations include the American Institute of Nutrition, the American Society of Cell Biology, and the Institute of Food Technologists. He has published over one hundred articles and papers on food, nutrition, and health.

The Research Center contains approximately 40,000 square feet of laboratory space and has some of the world's most advanced instrumentation for nutritional analysis and nutritional determination. "Many of the big pharmaceutical laboratories do a lot of different determinations," Jim Scala explains, "but we specialize. As a result, we can do such things as determine vitamin C quantities in the blood and urine perhaps better than any of these laboratories." It is here that research is conducted that will identify the food supplements of tomorrow—the next generation of Shaklee products.

Shaklee's commitment to developing products with the most solid scientific rationale has undoubtedly been a factor in attracting outstanding scientists to the Research Center. The Center's professionals include people with advanced degrees in chemistry, nutrition, microbiology, analytical chemistry, pharmaceutical chemistry, health science, process engineering, and packaging engineering.

The Center's advanced equipment makes it possible for the research staff to work with materials in precise and sophisticated ways. Jim explains that working with nature has a somewhat different meaning today than in the past. For example, the scanning electron microscope can magnify raw ingredient samples up to 100,000 times. "This allows us to monitor the variations in nutrient quality that occur in natural ingredients. These can be affected by soil conditions, rainfall, and other natural phenomena. I think harmony with nature means that our product delivers something that makes the body function more effectively. So it's no longer just a matter of the selection of ingredients but of the juxtaposition of one ingredient with another. It takes a great deal of serious engineering to accomplish this successfully.

"In some instances, we can actually improve on Nature. For example, we've determined that there are five different components of dietary fiber, and of course it's hard for people to get all of them in their diets. Well, in our fiber products we've been able to bring all five components of dietary fiber together. In a sense, this is improving on Nature, and yet it's compatible with our concept of harmony with Nature. This is just one illustration of what we can do today that couldn't be done in the past."

Shaklee products use only natural flavoring and vegetable coloring, such as beet powder; and no artificial sweeteners are used. Scientists sometimes find that the addition of a man-made ingredient can make a natural product even better. Perhaps the clearest example of this is Shaklee's Instant Protein. The soy protein used in the product is the best available, but soy is naturally deficient in one amino acid, methionine. Shaklee therefore adds DL-methionine, which the body is capable of metabolizing fully, so that Instant Protein provides a complete protein. "This process enables us to borrow the best of man, which is the DL-methionine," Jim explains, "and combine it with the best of Nature, which is the soy protein after we've removed all the extraneous materials." This combination of modern knowledge with natural ingredients is a good example of what can be done today—and still be in harmony with Nature.

In nutrition, as in the other sciences, major breakthroughs occur irregularly and infrequently, and are brought about not by luck but, as Jim Scala says, "by plain hard work." At the Research Center, the emphasis is on developing new products to meet genuine nutrition needs and on improving existing products. The research is painstaking and often tedious. A significant portion of the Center's work focuses on developing quality-control procedures. Products are analyzed and tested hundreds of times. A batch of Vita-Lea, for instance, is given 262 quality-control tests. As many as 172 quality tests are performed on certain raw materials.

Shaklee also conducts clinical tests to prove product claims, to provide the basis for new product development, and to extend the nutrition knowledge base. The results of several studies have been delivered at important professional meetings, including the American Medical Association's annual convention.

Gary Shansby has said that Shaklee's future will be built on a solid scientific foundation, and the work at the Research Center supports this statement. "We're committed to excellence," the CEO emphasizes. "If we can't find the best raw material, we'll delay the introduction of a product. If the research shows that the product just doesn't live up to its promise, we won't introduce it at all. We want a perfect product, and we won't settle for less. If it's not the best, it won't be sold." These are not idle words. Shaklee has indeed taken certain products off the market temporarily because the available raw materials didn't come up to the company's standards.

Although Shaklee stresses that its independent contractors be knowledgeable on nutrition, it insists that salespeople do not prescribe nutritional programs. In fact, people have been terminated for attempting this. Instead, the person-to-person presentation explains the basic facts about nutrition, so that the individual can select the product that fits his personal needs.

The U.S. Recommended Daily Allowance for nutrients can be a useful guideline for people analyzing their own diets. It should be emphasized, however, that the government's recommendations are merely guidelines. The Shaklee line of more than forty Nutritional Products includes two products that, taken together, form what the company calls "nutritional insurance." Four Vita-Lea tablets along with one ounce of Instant Protein taken in milk or juice provide all the U.S. RDA nutrients. This combination is the one most frequently ordered by people just beginning to use Shaklee food supplements. Nutritional needs, obviously, are as individual as fingerprints and depend upon such things as age, sex, occupation, and level of physical activity.

Even though contemporary food habits seem to result in inadequate nutrition for many people, the potential for improvement has never been better. Today anyone can educate himself, learn his individual needs, and program his own "nutritional insurance." Many Shaklee people testify that improved nutrition has led not just to better health for them but to more energy and increased enjoyment of life.

"You know, people sometimes say you can't expect to feel terrific after a certain age," Jim Scala says thoughtfully. "I think that's wrong. You can. It ultimately comes down to what you want to do with you life.

"Your health is dependent upon three things: genetics, environment, and lifestyle. There is nothing you can do about your ancestors, but you can certainly exercise some control over your environment and lifestyle. Nutrition is one of the most important aspects of your life. And, fortunately, you have the freedom to make the choices that will lead to good health."

13

Shaklee, Today and Tomorrow

IN THE 1960s, as Shaklee continued its rapid growth, it became impossible for Dr. Shaklee, Forrest, Jr., and Lee to oversee every phase of the business personally as they once had. The one-time family business had become a corporation, and it was necessary, the partners realized, to bring in professional management to lead it. The Shaklees recognized that the talents needed to build a business from the ground up are not the same as those needed to run a large corporation.

"All three of us were jacks of all trades," Forrest says. "During the early years we knew every facet of the business. But there finally came a point when it was just too large, and we had to hire specialists and rely on their expertise."

Lee compares the company's growth during the late '60s and early '70s to human adolescence. "When the business enters its adolescent years, that's the most difficult stage of all. A business experiences its growing pains, just as an adolescent does.

"We weren't immune from errors. It was very trying to make the transition from a family-operated business to a viable corporation managed by professionals. When we brought a lot of new people aboard in the early '70s, it was only to be expected that some of them would be poor selections and would have to be replaced. We discovered in the process that nobody is irreplaceable—and that includes the three of us."

As Shaklee attracted outside professional management, the new executives quickly became dedicated to upholding the Shaklee philosophy. Forrest and Lee have remained on the Board of Directors. "Every so often," Forrest explains, "the other members of the Board of Directors lean over to Lee or me and ask, 'How will that suit the family philosophy?' Over the last few years we've expounded on that enough so that I feel our management knows the philosophy. We never worry about them stepping outside those guidelines."

In their attempts to attract top management, the Shaklees didn't allow their egos to interfere with the company's best interests. Recruiting was a slow business, but when the right person showed up for a job, that person was hired.

J. Gary Shansby, the present Chief Executive Officer, is a good example of this hiring philosophy. Gary had an impeccable background, and the three Shaklees recognized that the then thirty-seven-year-old executive would fit in perfectly with the Shaklee business.

Yet Gary almost didn't join Shaklee. When he first encountered the company, he had reached a point in his career where he was disenchanted with corporate life and had tentatively decided to leave the world of big business to become an entrepreneur. He hoped to buy a small company and build it up, using everything he had learned during his corporate career.

Gary had a meteoric rise in the corporate world. After his graduation from the University of Washington in 1959, he had been recruited by Colgate Palmolive, where he earned a series of rapid promotions. In 1967 he left Colgate to join American Home Products, and by the time he was thirty he was President of one of the company's subsidiaries located in San Francisco. American Home wanted to transfer Gary to New York in 1971, but Gary preferred to stay in California.

He moved to the Clorox Company in Oakland, where he became Vice President in Charge of Acquisitions.

Gary became more and more disenchanted with the formal atmosphere and bureaucracy of large corporations, though he realized he had learned a lot in that atmosphere. He had learned creative marketing, how to take risks, how to go for market share, and the necessity of making a superior product. Most importantly, he had learned that a business exists to earn income for its owners, the shareholders. As he puts it, he had learned "the bottom line."

In 1973 Gary decided to join the San Francisco office of Booz, Allen & Hamilton, one of the world's largest and most prestigious consulting firms. Having come into the firm as a partner, he worked on strategic planning with such consumer-products companies as Pillsbury, Olympia Brewing, H. J. Heinz, Nestlé, and Libby, McNeill & Libby.

As exciting as it was to work closely with many of the nation's leading corporations, Gary was spending 80 percent of his time away from his family; his continual consulting trips required him to leave the San Francisco area on trips to the East. Therefore he decided to strike out on his own. He would find a consulting client in the Bay Area so that he could spend some time there. And while he looked for this client, he would keep his eyes open for a $4 or $5 million company he could buy.

In checking into several consumer-products companies in the area, Gary came across Shaklee. From what he could see, the company was at a stage in its development where his consulting services could be valuable. Within two weeks of being introduced to the head of personnel, Gary had been called into the President's office and told that he was being considered as a candidate for the position of Executive Vice President of U.S. Operations.

Gary recounts, "I reminded them that I was offering consulting services—not looking for a job. I was interested in what I was doing, and didn't want to go to work for another company."

Gary met with Dr. Shaklee, Forrest, and Lee. Each of them asked him to reconsider his decision. "Oh, I hit it off with all three of them," Gary notes. "Dr. Shaklee had both a scientific background and a philosophy that I found intriguing. I'd been working with companies that talked policy, and here was a man who talked philosophy—and under his leadership the company had prospered.

"Forrest was a very warm human being, with a likable kind of old-shoe personality, a straightforward man who said what he thought. And Lee was a man with a strong, forceful personality, very good in sales promotion."

Interested, Gary researched Shaklee further. "The company really seriously believed in helping others. It was not the typical tough, competitive environment. But I was frankly skeptical about the statement on the labels of Shaklee products, 'The name that is a stamp of quality.' A lot of companies say that, but it's just talk. But when I checked out Shaklee products, I found they were as natural as they could possibly be at the time. It was a good product line."

The other factors that influenced Gary's final decision were personal. One was his long-standing desire to be located in Northern California. Another was his own belief in physical fitness and good health. And he wanted to share in a company's profits; this was solved when it was decided that stock would be made available to Gary so that he could participate in the profits.

Dr. Shaklee said the company was looking for a man like Gary, who could provide high-level management with a human touch. And he convinced Gary that he was looking for a company like Shaklee. In March 1975 Gary joined as Executive Vice President and Chief Operating Officer. Two months later he was elected a Director, and that September he was named President. In May 1976, fourteen months after he joined Shaklee, Gary became Chief Executive Officer.

The company was not without its problems. It had grown so fast that some systems were unwieldy and inefficient. Delivery of orders was slow. Shaklee had overextended itself overseas. New people were coming on board, both in the home office and in the sales force, faster than they could be trained.

Gary's first task was to assess the situation. "It became apparent to me that the field organization was Shaklee's greatest asset. They have great inspiration and great dedication. They are very independent, which is a strength in this company. And they are very loyal. But many people were feeling frustrated, and some were becoming disillusioned due to our internal problems.

"I quickly formulated three priorities," Gary recalls. "And improving service to salespeople topped the list.

"My second priority was to recruit top quality management. I wanted people with experience in direct sales who understood how to market quality products."

Gary's third priority was to recruit outsiders for the Board of Directors, people who would bring objectivity to long-range policy decisions.

Moving on all three fronts was incredibly complex. "I don't think anyone could have experienced more trying times during his first year as CEO," Gary explains.

However, his efforts paid off. When Gary joined the company in 1975, Shaklee's sales were $80 million. His first year as Chief Executive Officer, 1976, was a good year for Shaklee. Sales increased and earnings went up fourfold. The price of Shaklee stock reached a new high, and the company began to receive favorable attention from the financial community.

What changes had been made that year? The improvement in the quality of service to the sales force had been dramatic. When Gary arrived, the time between when an order was placed and when it was delivered had been as long as six or seven weeks. In 1976 it was reduced to sixteen days (and today it has been reduced to eight days).

Also, Gary and his team analyzed Shaklee International,

as explained in Chapter 4, and decided to focus efforts on the United Kingdom, Canada, and Japan, rather than entering several mainland European markets. New outside board members also joined the company. Several new officers were recruited including Jack Wilder, Vice President of Sales. Jack represents the new breed of experienced executive on the Shaklee team today. Jack has an extensive background in direct selling that includes working with Mary Kay Cosmetics in Dallas as Vice President of Sales. He had previously worked for IBM, where he was one of the company's top salespersons.

Other problems loomed. In 1974 Shaklee's main plant was destroyed by an explosion. Shaklee had been forced to hurriedly construct a plant in Hayward, California. That plant, while attractive, lacked the potential for long-range growth. In 1977 the decision was made to move. A large new plant would be a high-risk venture, but the decision to go ahead was a statement of faith in Shaklee's future.

Oklahoma was chosen as the site of the new plant for several reasons. It was close to the source of supply for the raw ingredients of most of the products. Distribution would be cost-efficient. Moreover, Oklahoma was very interested in having Shaklee and, as a right-to-work state, offered a climate suitable to the Shaklee management style of bringing employees into the decision-making process.

Designing the plant was a challenge. The decision was made not to cut corners. The Shaklee image of quality would be represented both in the architecture of the building and in the machinery inside the building. The $50 million plant was officially opened in October 1979. It is considered the best tableting facility in the world. And there is plenty of room for growth: seven football fields would fit under its roof.

As Shaklee outgrew its manufacturing facilities, the home-office staff expanded at such a rate that they were spread out in fourteen buildings in the East Bay Area. Something had to be done about that. After much deliberation, the company made a commitment to build a new home office in downtown San Francisco. Design work for 444 Market Street, Shaklee Terraces, began.

More changes began in 1977. Shaklee made a huge commitment to science and technology, and within the next four years increased its R and D investment from about $500,000 to over $7 million.

Management attention was turned to developing more sophisticated internal systems. Cliff Shaklee, Forrest's son, who had an accounting background, had set up the company's first computer system in the early '60s, using an IBM 402. He eventually managed its team of operators, programmers, and systems analysts. In 1977 a new 2003 Alpine computer system was installed to handle everything from payroll to bonus recaps.

Also that year the company concentrated on upgrading field training programs and convention planning. All in all, it was a good year for Shaklee. The company's steady growth indicated that the new programs were working and the decisions were sound.

But in 1978, after two prosperous years, Shaklee sales suddenly flattened out. Gary and his staff analyzed what had happened. "That was some learning experience. I got a ten-year education in direct selling in a single year. We just hadn't listened to our sales organization as carefully as we should have, and we'd raised prices a little too much. I think it was overconfidence—things had been going too well. But the field organization was wonderful. Their spirits never wavered, nor did their respect for the company. So in spite of our shortcomings, we came out of it with flying colors."

The following year, as domestic sales recovered, international sales took a gratifying leap. The growth was most dramatic in Japan, while Canada also made good progress. But Gary knew another big change had to be made.

In May 1980, in thirty-three cities across the United States, 15,000 Sales Leaders gathered to watch a special film in which Gary announced the new direction Shaklee was taking. The

Board of Directors had decided to refocus on Nutritional Products, where there seemed to be the greatest potential for growth. In order to do this, Shaklee's line of household and personal care products was cut from 178 to 42 stockkeeping units.

Gary explained that Nutritional Products were the best door openers and business builders for Distributors. He argued that the smaller line would enable Sales Leaders to manage their cash flow more easily, which in turn would strengthen their businesses. The remaining non-nutritional products would be the most popular ones. And Shaklee's emphasis would be on nutrition, as it had been when the company began.

The change was not well received. Sales Leaders wrote or called to express their disapproval. "I thought that time would prove it was a good decision, and that the people who initially dissented would agree with the change," Gary said. "But the reaction was so dramatic!" The next day Mount Saint Helens erupted, and one executive, knowing that Gary hailed from Washington, wondered out loud which had created the greater explosion, Gary or the volcano.

By the time a year had passed, however, the waters had calmed. Shaklee's sales at home and abroad continued to climb. It was clear that the company's focus on nutrition was the right choice.

Over the years Shaklee's products and product line have changed often—and no doubt will continue to change. Gary points out that Shaklee's investment in research is proof of the company's commitment to meet future challenges. "And we never sacrifice a single thing for temporary savings," he asserts, "because we know it will come back to haunt us in the long run."

Shaklee is well on its way to becoming the largest direct selling company in the United States. Trends suggest that a time may come when Shaklee is to nutrition what Procter & Gamble is to soap, what IBM is to computers. If current international sales are any indication, this success will extend into still more countries. More than likely, the company's focus on health will lead to expansion of the product line beyond nutrition and into other health products.

Despite the present size of the field organization, there is still tremendous untapped potential for Shaklee just in this country.

Financial World has stated that during the 1970s Shaklee was the number two company on the New York Stock Exchange in terms of sales potential. This statement was based on Shaklee's incredible gain in sales, from $20 million in 1970 to $314 million in 1979. The following year, sales volume was $411 million, an amazing increase of 31 percent. In 1981 sales moved still higher, toward the half-billion-dollar mark.

Shaklee's future has never looked brighter. The company, in spite of its growth, has retained its unique philosophy and the family spirit that built it. The words Dr. Shaklee spoke so often during the company's infancy still apply: "You ain't seen nothin' yet!"

Appendix

The Shaklee Sales Organization and Sales Plan

Starting with the entry level position and ending with the highest rank, the sales structure of Shaklee is as follows: Distributor, Assistant Supervisor, Supervisor, Coordinator, Key Coordinator, and Master Coordinator.

DISTRIBUTOR

A Distributor (the entry level position) is an independent contractor, in business for himself. To become a Shaklee Distributor one is required to fill out an application and purchase a "New Distributor Kit." The current price for the kit is under $15.00. The application can be obtained from anyone in the sales organization. The person from whom the application is obtained becomes the new Distributor's sponsor.

The new Distributor has the right to purchase Shaklee Products at their wholesale price, which averages 35 percent less than Shaklee's suggested retail price. The Distributor can sell the products at the suggested retail price or he can establish his own retail price. There are no territorial restrictions placed on the Distributor. He can sell anywhere and to anyone except Distributors in other sales groups.

Profits to the Distributor are derived in several ways: The direct profit, the profit earned on Purchase Volume, and the profit earned by sponsoring new Distributors.

The Direct Profit. This is the spread between the cost of the products to the Distributor and the price he receives.

The Profit on Purchase Volume (PV). This is a dollar and cents amount that's credited to the Distributor for each wholesale purchase he makes (Personal PV).

Cash bonuses, awards and other incentives are based on the Distributor's monthly PV. The bonus rate of his PV increases as his volume increases. Only active Distributors who have minimum monthly personal PV of at least $150 are eligible to earn cash bonuses on personal and group PV, which starts at 3 percent. PV of at least $300 earns a 6 percent bonus, and when the volume reaches $600, the bonus increases to 8 percent. These monthly bonuses are paid by the Distributor's Assistant Supervisor or Supervisor.

The Profit Earned on PV of Sponsored Distributors. Every Distributor is encouraged to sponsor new Distributors. The people he recruits are often friends, family, colleagues and, most often, satisfied customers. The advantage of sponsoring is great, because the PV earned by those he sponsored becomes part of the sponsor's group PV—which of course increases his bonuses.

When a Distributor's personal and group monthly PV reaches $1,000, he moves up the sales organization's structure to—

ASSISTANT SUPERVISOR

When he reaches this level with a monthly PV of $1,000, his bonus rate increases to 11 percent. And it jumps to 14 percent when the monthly PV increases to at least $1,500. This, of course, is in addition to his Direct Profit, which is approximately 35 percent of his own total monthly sales. As Assistant Supervisor he helps conduct sales meetings for the Distributors he sponsored, becomes their supplier of Shaklee Products, and pays them monthly cash bonuses. This often means he has to set up a Shaklee office in his home, as he must keep the necessary records to calculate the bonuses of his sales group. The next step up the ladder is to—

SUPERVISOR

For an Assistant Supervisor to advance to this level, his group must produce sales that generate $2,000 in PV for two consecutive months and $3,000 in the third month. And his group must maintain the $3,000 level in order for him to retain his position. There is strong motivation to reach and hold on to this position. For one thing, his bonus is increased to 22 percent. He can qualify for monthly credits toward the use of a Shaklee bonus car. He's invited to the New Supervisors Convention in San Francisco, at the company's expense. And after being a Supervisor for six consecutive months he becomes eligible for group insurance at low premium rates.

His responsibilities expand as well. He conducts sales meetings, maintains records, and distributes bonuses and inventory to Assistant Supervisors and Distributors in his group. As a Sales Leader he now deals directly with the home office and can call upon the Supervisor Counselors for help and to exchange ideas.

As the Supervisor builds his Shaklee business, he will help his Distributors and Assistant Supervisors to reach the rank of Supervisor. It's to his advantage to have as many Supervisors as possible develop out of his sales group. As his people become Supervisors the relationship changes. He is now paid a special leadership bonus, directly from Shaklee, based on the new Supervisor's group PV. The monthly bonus he receives is 5 percent of the new group's PV. Each time a member of his sales group advances to the rank of Supervisor, he receives another monthly bonus based on their production. Of course, that's in addition to his own Direct Profit and the 22 percent he receives from the PV of his own group.

There's more. He can earn money on the production of three levels of Supervisors. Let's explain this with an example. Al is a Supervisor. Betty, a Distributor in his sales group, moves up the ladder to the rank of Supervisor. To Al, Betty is now a First Level Supervisor and he receives a 5 percent bonus based on her group's PV. Carl is a Distributor in Betty's group. When Carl becomes a Supervisor, he becomes a Second Level Supervisor to Al. So in addition to the 5 percent he receives from Betty's group's production, he now receives 2 percent based on the sales of Carl's group. (Betty receives 5 percent.)

Let's go on. Diane is a Distributor in Carl's sales group. When she becomes a Supervisor, she is a First Level Supervisor to Carl, a Second Level Supervisor to Betty and a Third Level Supervisor to Al. Al receives a monthly bonus of 1 percent based on the production of Diane's group.

At this point Al receives in earnings the following:

On his own sales—approximately 35% Direct Profit
On his group's production—22% based on the group's PV plus 1% for
    cash = total of 23%
On Betty's group—5% based on their PV (1st Level Supervisor)
On Carl's group—2% based on their PV (2nd Level Supervisor)
On Diane's group—1% based on their PV (3rd Level Supervisor)

The next step up the sales organization's ladder is Coordinator.

COORDINATOR

To become a Coordinator, a Supervisor must develop four First Level Supervisors from his sales group of Distributors. Now he will receive an extra ½ percent special Coordinator bonus. He can also select a more luxurious bonus car, such as a Cadillac or Lincoln Continental. After he develops a fifth First Level Supervisor, the company will gradually decrease the PV requirements for his personal sales group below $3,000, to give him more time to work with his growing sales organization. (Few Coordinators have monthly PV below $3,000, however.) Once a Coordinator has held this rank in good standing for twelve consecutive months, he is eligible to apply for transfer to a reduced activity status, which provides residual bonus checks equal to 50 percent of the bonuses he would have received had he remained active. Although this is a generous plan, only a small percentage of eligible Coordinators do elect reduced activity status; many choose to remain active long after they have become eligible for Social Security.

The Coordinator who develops nine First Levels (remember, these are people sponsored in his personal sales group who have become Supervisors) is promoted to Key Coordinator.

KEY COORDINATOR

A Key has the freedom to concentrate on developing his sales group; he has no required minimum PV. Keys who prefer to operate as managers no longer have to be involved with day-to-day details of inventory. Many, however, elect to set up offices and to maintain their personal group PV as an example for their sponsorship group. By the same token, many Keys continue to sponsor and develop in order to increase the number of their First Levels.

MASTER COORDINATOR

The Key who develops fifteen First Levels has reached the top ranks in the Shaklee sales force. If the company concurs that he demonstrates excellence in both sales and leadership, he becomes a *Master Coordinator.* He is entitled to a free bonus car from a list of luxury cars—with no PV requirements. As long as he maintains fifteen First Levels, he will be entitled to this car. As a Master he is also entitled to attend free of charge all International Coordinators Conventions, again with no PV requirement. Masters at this level often earn annual incomes in six figures.